W9-AVM-106

CHOCOLATE!

Good Housekeeping FAVORITE RECIPES

CHOCOLATE!

Good Housekeeping FAVORITE RECIPES

HEARST BOOKS
A DIVISION OF STERLING PUBLISHING CO., INC.
NEW YORK

Copyright © 2005 by
Hearst Communications, Inc.

All rights reserved. The recipes and photographs
in this volume are intended for the personal use
of the reader and may be reproduced for that
purpose only. Any other use, especially
commercial use, is forbidden under law without
the written permission of the copyright holder.

Ellen Levine	**Editor in Chief**
Susan Westmoreland	**Food Director**
Susan Deborah Goldsmith	**Associate Food Director**
Delia Hammock	**Nutrition Director**
Sharon Franke	**Food Appliances Director**
Richard Eisenberg	**Special Projects Director**
Marilu Lopez	**Art Director**

**Library of Congress
Cataloging-in-Publication Data**
Chocolate! : good housekeeping favorite recipes
/ the editors of Good housekeeping.
p. cm.
Includes index.
ISBN 1-58816-440-3
1. Cookery (Chocolate) 2. Chocolate.
I. Good housekeeping.
TX767.C5C4817 2004
641.6'374--dc22
2004009573
10 9 8 7 6 5 4

Book design by Renato Stanisic

Photography Credits
Sang An: Page 215
Peter Ardito: Pages 175, 182
James Baigrie: Page 119
Mary Ellen Bartley: Page 122
Brian Hagiwara: Pages 8, 31, 143, 165, 229
Rita Maas: Pages 3, 37, 57, 117, 125, 127, 128,
133, 136, 185, 219
Steven Mark Needham: Pages 6, 16, 20, 76, 93,
155, 168, 195, 220, 231, 232, 233, 234, 235, 236
Alan Richardson: Pages 29, 95, 101, 134, 151
Ann Stratton: Pages 49, 78, 84, 89,
176, 187, 188, 199
Mark Thomas: Pages 2, 22, 27, 45, 46, 53, 54, 108,
112, 141, 147, 190, 196, 202, 207, 217

Published by Hearst Books
A Division of Sterling Publishing Co., Inc.
387 Park Avenue South, New York, NY 10016

Good Housekeeping and Hearst Books are
trademarks of Hearst Communications, Inc.

The Good Housekeeping Cookbook Seal
guarantees that the recipes in this cookbook meet
the strict standards of the Good Housekeeping
Institute, a source of reliable information and a
consumer advocate since 1900. Every recipe
has been triple-tested for ease, reliability,
and great taste.

www.goodhousekeeping.com

Distributed in Canada by Sterling Publishing
c/o Canadian Manda Group, 165 Dufferin Street
Toronto, Ontario, Canada M6K 3H6

Distributed in Australia by Capricorn Link
(Australia) Pty. Ltd.
P.O. Box 704, Windsor, NSW 2756 Australia

Manufactured in China

ISBN 1-58816-440-3

For information about custom editions, special sales,
premium and corporate purchases, please contact
Sterling Special Sales Department at 800-805-5489
or specialsales@sterlingpub.com.

CONTENTS

FOREWORD

J ust talking about doing a chocolate cookbook raised the level of excitement in our test kitchens. As we looked at favorite chocolate recipes from the magazine and reminisced about every chocolate dessert we'd ever loved, it became clear that we were a group of—well—chocoholics.

We did have moments when all things chocolate were not sweet. When it came to the perfect chocolate layer cake we disagreed, almost violently, on the proper frosting. The Seven-Minute fans in the crowd couldn't abide buttercream and the buttercream contingent couldn't imagine anything as insubstantial as "marshmallow" on rich chocolatey layers. We have taken the bipartisan approach and included both frostings as well as others, including my son's favorite, Peanut Butter Frosting.

Whether you are someone who keeps a stash of chocolate cookies in your desk to sate afternoon cravings or one who occasionally indulges in a Molten Chocolate Cake, *Chocolate!* has something to delight you. You'll find cakes from the easiest One-Bowl Chocolate Cake to Chocolate Pound Cake with Irish Whiskey Cream Sauce. Satisfy your brownie cravings with Peanut Butter Swirl, Black Forest, or my all-time favorite, Chocolate-Hazelnut Brownies. Lunchbox carriers will love triple Chocolate Chubbies, Chocolate Mint Sandwich Cookies, and Chocolate Crinkles. For a kids' get together, try Whoopie Pies or Rich Chocolate Cupcakes with Malted-Milk Frosting. In addition to fabulous recipes, *Chocolate!* is filled with great tips to make your sweets look and taste wonderful. All 160 recipes have been triple-tested in the GH test kitchens by our chocolate-loving staff, so they're guaranteed to be good.

—Susan Westmoreland

FOOD DIRECTOR, *Good Housekeeping*

INTRODUCTION
Chocolate—"Food of the Gods"

This book is for chocolate lovers who covet rich, fudgy brownies studded with crunchy walnuts; warm, fragrant chocolate cake with melt-in-your-mouth molten centers; or moist, mile-high devil's food layer cake filled with silky chocolate buttercream and festooned with chocolate curls. Our recipes are a collection of unabashedly rich, tempting, and sometimes downright decadent ways to enjoy chocolate, the "food of the gods." For many of us, a day without a chocolate treat is a day without sunshine; while for others, chocolate is a greatly anticipated and slowly savored occasional indulgence. Our intent is to deliver chocolate at its very best, whether in Caramel-Nut Brownies, Old-Fashioned Cocoa Cake, Double Chocolate-Chunk Cookies, or Rocky Road Ice Cream Cake. We have included quick and easy recipes that can be prepared in mere minutes and others that are meant to fill a rainy afternoon. All of our recipes are written in the easy-to-follow, step-by-step *Good Housekeeping* style, so they will turn out perfect time after time, whether you are just learning your way around the kitchen or can "cook with your eyes closed."

Chocolate: A Short History
Chocolate is commonly considered a modern-day sweet, but it has been around for several thousand years. Early on, the Mayas learned how to grow, harvest, ferment, roast, and grind cocoa seeds into a paste. The paste was mixed with water, chile peppers, and cornmeal and enjoyed as a bitter drink. By 1400, the Aztecs were trading with the Mayas for cocoa and

used cocoa seeds and beans as currency. The Aztecs readily embraced the Mayas' bitter chocolate drink, but they considered it so special that it was reserved for rulers, priests, and decorated soldiers. The people of the court adored the drink, and it was common for as many as fifty portions of the *xocolatl* (pronounced shoco-latel) to be consumed in a day.

History was made in 1519, when Montezuma greeted the Spanish explorer Hernán Cortes with a goblet of the revered bitter chocolate brew. It didn't take long for Cortes to succumb to the drink's charms. He returned to Spain nine years later with cocoa seeds and the knowledge of how to turn them into the valuable paste. In Spain, the drink became all the rage at the court of King Charles V, where it was prepared with sugar and served hot.

By the mid-1600s, drinking chocolate had become a delightful habit in much of Western Europe, as Italian and French visitors to Spain spread word of its charm. In London, an enterprising merchant opened the first of many chocolate houses, and before long, the Dutch were sending cocoa beans to America. In the 1700s, chocolate beverages were being sold as restoratives in Boston, and by 1765 James Baker had opened the first—and now oldest—chocolate company in America.

From this time forward, chocolate improved in leaps and bounds. The Austrians found that chocolate paste could be used to produce cakes. And in the 1800s, the Dutch figured out how to extract the cocoa butter from chocolate, thereby creating unsweetened cocoa, which became a baking staple. In England, the availability of cocoa butter led to the creation of simple and delicious chocolate candy. Candy bars appeared in England by the mid-1800s, but it wasn't until nearly the end of the century that Rudolphe Lindt invented the process that resulted in the creamier, smoother chocolate that became known as Swiss chocolate.

Today's desserts and confections are a far cry from the first bitter chocolate drink that was enjoyed more than four hundred years ago. We live in a time where there are chocolates and chocolate desserts to suit every mood, every taste, and every occasion.

How Chocolate Is Made

In a way chocolate *does* grow on trees, the cacao tree, whose botanical name is *Theobroma cacao*, from the Greek for "food of the gods." Cacao trees need three things to thrive: high temperature, high humidity, and a special insect that pollinates its flowers. The flowers that do not produce fruit develop large pods that contain cocoa beans. The beans are removed from the pods and placed in piles to ferment, after which they are left in the sun to dry. The cocoa beans are then roasted and their papery husks removed by gently crushing the beans into little, irregular pieces known as nibs. The nibs are ground, and the fat they contain—cocoa butter—is then liquefied. The whole mixture is turned into a mass called chocolate liquor, which despite its name is a solid and does not contain alcohol. The chocolate liquor is then used to make cocoa and chocolate for all the world to enjoy.

Types of Chocolate

Unsweetened chocolate is simply ground cocoa beans. Professionals call it chocolate liquor. It is harsh and bitter tasting and is never eaten out of hand. It is most often used in baking in combination with semisweet chocolate

Bittersweet chocolate has been sweetened, but the amount of sugar varies from brand to brand. Some bittersweet chocolates list the percentage of chocolate liquor: a chocolate with 70 percent is more bitter and has a more intense flavor than one with 64 percent.

Semisweet chocolate is similar to bittersweet chocolate, although it is usually a bit sweeter. It can be used interchangeably with bittersweet chocolate in most recipes. It is available in 1-ounce squares, in small bars, and in bulk at specialty food stores.

German's sweet chocolate, used to make German chocolate cake, is sold under a brand name and should not be confused with bittersweet or semisweet chocolate.

Milk chocolate contains dried milk powder and a high percentage of sugar. It is essentially an eating chocolate—it's not usually used for baking.

White chocolate is not really chocolate at all but rather vanilla-flavored sweetened cocoa butter (a by-product of chocolate processing), although some mid-priced brands substitute vegetable fat for the cocoa butter.

Unsweetened cocoa is what provides the rich chocolate flavor in many desserts. There are two kinds of cocoa powder: natural and Dutch-process. In baking, the two are not interchangeable. Natural cocoa has a full, rich flavor and is the type most commonly used in American kitchens. It is always combined with baking soda. Dutch-process cocoa is treated with an alkali that reduces its acidity. It gives baked goods a rich dark color and it doesn't need to be combined with baking soda. For a hot cup of cocoa, use your favorite.

Chocolate Basics

Storing Chocolate Chocolate is best stored in a cool, dry place, such as a pantry. Or wrap the chocolate in an airtight heavy plastic bag and place in the crisper drawer of your refrigerator. To prevent the chocolate from developing condensation, let it come to room temperature while still wrapped before chopping or breaking it up. If chocolate is stored at warmer temperatures, it may develop a "bloom" (the cocoa butter rising to the surface), which are grayish streaks. Chocolate that has developed a bloom is perfectly fine to melt and use in cooking or baking.

Chopping Chocolate Use a large chef's knife or heavy serrated knife to cut chocolate into pieces. Be sure to use a perfectly clean and dry cutting board. To finely chop chocolate, cut it into small pieces (about 1/4 inch) by hand, then pulse it in a food processor fitted with the metal blade until finely chopped.

Melting Chocolate There is a simple rule when it comes to melting chocolate: keep the heat low and the chocolate dry. Even one tiny drop of water can cause the chocolate to "seize up" (stiffen), which ruins it. There are two easy ways to melt chocolate: in the microwave or in a double boiler or bowl set over simmering water. It is not a good idea to melt chocolate in a saucepan unless the chocolate is combined with other ingredients such as cream or butter and the saucepan is heavy.

Before melting chocolate, always chop or break it into little pieces (about 1/4 inch) so it can melt quickly and evenly. To melt chocolate on the stovetop place it in a bowl on top of a double boiler set over—not in—a pan containing about 1 1/2 inches of simmering water set over low heat. Stir occasionally with a heat-safe spatula until the chocolate is melted and smooth, then set the bowl on the counter. To melt chocolate in a microwave, place the chopped chocolate in a microwave-safe bowl. Heat it on Low or Medium-Low power at 30-second intervals, stirring, to see if the chocolate has melted. When chocolate is melted in the microwave, it continues to hold its shape even when melted.

Kitchen Basics

You do not have to be an experienced cook to turn out fabulous chocolate desserts. The key to success is three-fold: use the right ingredients, measure them accurately, and use the proper equipment. Keep this in mind and you are guaranteed to turn out perfect chocolate desserts time after time. All of the recipes in this book have been triple-tested in the *Good Housekeeping* kitchens. Be sure to read a recipe in its entirety to familiarize yourself with it before you begin. Make sure you have all of the necessary ingredients on hand. And do not substitute ingredients or baking pans unless the recipe so indicates.

Ingredient Know-How

Butter vs. Margarine Many of our recipes offer the option of using butter or margarine. Butter is usually listed first as it will give you the most delicious flavor and texture. If you do use margarine, make sure it contains 80 percent fat. Do not substitute light margarine, vegetable-oil spreads, or whipped butter. Soften butter by letting it stand, still wrapped, at room temperature for about 30 minutes or just until pliable—not soft or melty. Cutting butter into small pieces will speed up the process.

Flour We use all-purpose or cake flour in most of our recipes: they are not interchangeable. All-purpose flour is a blend of hard and soft wheats. Cake flour is made from soft wheat, so it produces cakes with an especially delicate texture. Do not use self-rising flour; it already has salt and a leavener added.

Baking Powder and Baking Soda Baking powder is a blend of baking soda, cream of tartar, and cornstarch. Keep it tightly closed in a cool, dry place. It's a good idea to replace it every six months. Baking soda, also known as bicarbonate of soda, is used when a recipe contains an acid ingredient, such as buttermilk, molasses, yogurt, chocolate, or sour cream. Dutch-process cocoa does not have to be combined with baking soda, as Dutching reduces its acidity.

Yeast We use active dry yeast, which is sold in 1/4-ounce packets and in jars. Be sure to check the freshness date before you use it. *Tip:* If you are not sure that your yeast is still good, stir it into the amount of warm liquid called for in the recipe and add a good pinch of sugar. If the mixture bubbles up after several minutes, it is still good.

Eggs Our recipes call for "large" grade eggs. We do not recommend substituting a different size. Store eggs in their original container in the refrigerator.

Sugar Granulated white sugar is our baking basic. Superfine sugar dissolves very quickly, making it excellent for meringues. Confectioners' sugar (also called powdered sugar) is very finely ground and contains cornstarch. It is a good idea to sift it before use as it can be lumpy. Brown sugar (light and dark) is granulated sugar with some molasses added. Dark brown and light brown sugar are interchangeable in most of our recipes.

Measuring Know-How

If you measure ingredients correctly, you will have consistent baking results. In your kitchen you need liquid measuring cups (at least 1- and 2-cup), a set of nesting metal dry measuring cups, and a set of measuring spoons.

Liquids We recommend clear glass measuring cups. To measure a liquid accurately, place the cup on the counter and add the desired amount of liquid. Bend down to check the accuracy of the measure at eye level (do not lift up the cup).

Dry Ingredients To measure flour and sugar, first stir it with a fork or whisk to aerate it, as it tends to get packed down. Lightly spoon the flour into the measuring cup to overflowing, then level it off with a narrow metal spatula or the straight edge of a knife. To measure brown sugar or vegetable shortening, pack it firmly into the cup, then level it off. Butter does not need to be measured, as each stick is premarked with all of the measurements you will need. *Tip:* Before measuring sticky ingredients, such as corn syrup or honey, coat the inside of the liquid measuring cup with cooking spray and they will slide out easily.

Equipment Know-How

Time was, a sturdy bowl, a wooden spoon, and a rolling pin were all that was needed to turn out sweet treats. These days there seems to be almost limitless possibilities when it comes to baking equipment and tools, but the truth is, you only need a small number of carefully chosen items to get the job done well.

Electric mixer A portable hand mixer is all you need, but if you have a sturdy stand mixer, by all means use it.

Cake pans three 8- and 9-inch round pans

Metal baking pans 8- and 9-inch square pans and a 13" by 9" pan.

Glass or ceramic baking dishes Have several on hand, including 13" by 9", 10" by 15", and 11" by 7".

Other useful pans 10- and 12-cup Bundt pans, 9" by 3" and 10" by 2¼" springform pans, 9- and 10-inch tube pans, 9- and 11-inch removable-bottom tart pans, 9" by 5" and 8½" by 4½" loaf pans, 15" by 10" jelly-roll pans.

Basic tools mixing bowls, large heavy cookie sheets, wire cooling racks, regular and mini muffin pans, custard cups, heat-safe rubber spatula, wire whisk, parchment paper, pastry bags and tips, rolling pin, instant-read thermometer, pastry brush.

CAKES, COFFEE CAKES & BREADS

What comes to mind when you hear the word *cake*? Perhaps a luscious three-layer beauty frosted with smooth-as-silk chocolate buttercream or a cocoa-rich Bundt cake bursting with tiny shards of bittersweet chocolate. This chapter offers these time-honored sweets and more, including a Sacher Torte and an easy One-Bowl Chocolate Cake that's ideal when time is short. Also featured are some delicious coffee cakes and breads, perfect for serving alongside a hot cup of afternoon tea.

Perfect Cakes Every Time

Baking is a precise process that requires the correct ingredients, accurate measuring, and directions that must be followed to a tee.

Cake batter should be made with room-temperature ingredients. Remove butter, eggs, and dairy products from the refrigerator about thirty minutes ahead. Soften butter until it is malleable—not shiny and melting. Room-temperature eggs can be beaten to their greatest volume.

Most of our recipes call for all-purpose flour, but occasionally cake flour is used. If you don't have cake flour, here's an easy substitution: For every cup of flour, spoon 2 tablespoons cornstarch into a 1-cup measure. Spoon in enough bleached all-purpose flour to fill the cup, then level it off.

Pan Prep To line a pan, place it on a piece of waxed paper. Use a pencil to trace around the bottom of the pan, then cut out the round. To grease the pan, apply an even layer of vegetable shortening using a folded piece of paper towel. To flour the pan, sprinkle about 1 tablespoon of flour into the greased pan, then tilt it to coat the bottom and side; tap out the excess.

Oven Smarts Position the racks before turning on the oven and preheat thoroughly. Always use an oven thermometer. When baking a single cake or two layers, place them in the center of the oven. If baking more cakes, stagger them in the upper and lower third of the oven. Cakes baked in tube pans should be placed in the lower third of the oven.

Store It Refrigerate cakes that contain fillings or frostings made of dairy products. Unfrosted butter cakes can be stored at room temperature for about three days. Foam cakes dry out quickly; store at room temperature up to two days.

Old-Fashioned Chocolate Layer Cake

A tender triple-layer cake flavored with cocoa and frosted with an indulgent buttercream frosting.

PREP: 40 MINUTES PLUS COOLING   BAKE: 20 MINUTES
MAKES 16 SERVINGS

2 3/4 cups cake flour (not self-rising)
3/4 cup unsweetened cocoa
1 1/2 teaspoons baking soda
1/2 teaspoon salt
3/4 cup butter or margarine
   (1 1/2 sticks), softened

1 3/4 cups sugar
3 large eggs
1 1/2 teaspoons vanilla extract
1 1/2 cups milk
White Chocolate Buttercream
   Frosting (page 65)

1. Preheat oven to 350°F. Grease three 9-inch round cake pans. Line bottom of cake pans with waxed paper; grease and flour paper.

2. In large bowl, combine cake flour, cocoa, baking soda, and salt.

3. In large bowl, with mixer at medium speed, beat butter and sugar until light and fluffy, about 5 minutes.

4. Beat in eggs and vanilla until smooth, about 2 minutes. Reduce speed to low. Add flour mixture and milk; beat until combined. Increase speed to medium; beat 1 minute, occasionally scraping bowl.

5. Divide batter equally among prepared pans. Bake until toothpick inserted in center comes out clean, 20 to 25 minutes. Cool layers in pans on wire racks 10 minutes. Run thin knife around layers to loosen from sides of pans. Invert onto racks to cool completely.

6. Meanwhile, prepare White Chocolate Buttercream Frosting. Place one cake layer, rounded side up, on cake plate. With narrow metal spatula, spread 3/4 cup frosting over layer. Top with second layer, rounded side up. Spread remaining frosting over side and top of cake.

Each serving: About 500 calories, 5g protein, 65g carbohydrate, 26g total fat (16g saturated), 99mg cholesterol, 428mg sodium.

Classic Devil's Food Cake

Devil's food cake is a twentieth-century creation. No one knows for sure how the cake got its name, but many believe it was due to its dark color and richness—the opposite of light and delicate angel food cake.

PREP: 35 MINUTES PLUS COOLING   BAKE: 30 MINUTES
MAKES 16 SERVINGS

2 cups all-purpose flour

1 cup unsweetened cocoa

1 1/2 teaspoons baking soda

1/2 teaspoon salt

1/2 cup butter or margarine (1 stick), softened

1 cup packed light brown sugar

1 cup granulated sugar

3 large eggs

1 1/2 teaspoons vanilla extract

1 1/2 cups buttermilk

Rich Chocolate Frosting (page 59) or Fluffy White Frosting (page 69)

1. Preheat oven to 350°F. Grease three 8-inch round cake pans. Line bottoms with waxed paper; grease paper. Dust pans with flour.

2. In medium bowl, combine flour, cocoa, baking soda, and salt.

3. In large bowl, with mixer at low speed, beat butter and brown and granulated sugars until blended. Increase speed to high; beat until light and fluffy, about 5 minutes. Reduce speed to medium-low; add eggs, one at a time, beating well after each addition. Beat in vanilla. Add flour mixture alternately with buttermilk, beginning and ending with flour mixture; beat just until batter is smooth, occasionally scraping bowl with rubber spatula.

4. Divide batter equally among prepared pans; spread evenly. Place two pans on upper oven rack and one pan on lower oven rack so pans are not directly above one another. Bake until toothpick inserted in center comes out clean, 30 to 35 minutes. Cool layers in pans on wire rack 10 minutes. Run thin knife around layers to loosen from sides of pans. Invert onto racks. Remove waxed paper; cool completely.

5. Meanwhile, prepare Rich Chocolate Frosting. Place one cake layer, rounded side down, on cake plate. With narrow metal spatula, spread 1/3 cup frosting over layer. Top with second layer, rounded side up, and spread 1/3 cup frosting over layer. Place remaining layer, rounded side up, on top. Spread remaining frosting over side and top of cake.

Each serving: About 450 calories, 5g protein, 74g carbohydrate, 17g total fat (10g saturated), 72mg cholesterol, 355mg sodium.

Easy Chocolate-Buttermilk Cake

This cake is so delectably moist and chocolaty, it can be served without any frosting at all.

PREP: 30 MINUTES PLUS COOLING   BAKE: 30 MINUTES
MAKES 16 SERVINGS

2 1/4 cups all-purpose flour
3/4 cup unsweetened cocoa
1 3/4 cups sugar
2 teaspoons baking soda
1 1/4 teaspoons salt
1 1/2 cups buttermilk

1 cup vegetable oil
3 large eggs
1 1/2 teaspoons vanilla extract
White Chocolate Butter Frosting
(page 66)

1. Preheat oven to 350°F. Grease two 9-inch round cake pans or 10-inch Bundt pan. Dust pans with cocoa.

2. In large bowl, combine flour, cocoa, sugar, baking soda, and salt.

3. In medium bowl, with wire whisk, mix buttermilk, oil, eggs, and vanilla until blended. Add buttermilk mixture to flour mixture; whisk until smooth.

4. Divide batter equally between prepared pans; spread evenly. Bake until toothpick inserted in center comes out clean, about 30 minutes for 9-inch layers, or about 40 minutes for Bundt cake. Cool in pans on wire racks 10 minutes. Run thin knife around layers to loosen from sides of pan. Or, if using Bundt pan, run tip of knife around edge of cake to loosen. Invert onto racks to cool completely.

5. Meanwhile, prepare White Chocolate Butter Frosting. Place one layer, rounded side down, on cake plate. With narrow metal spatula, spread 2/3 cup frosting over layer. Top with second layer, rounded side up. Spread remaining frosting over side and top of cake.

Each serving: About 527 calories, 5g protein, 61g carbohydrate, 31g total fat (12g saturated), 72mg cholesterol, 505mg sodium.

One-Bowl Chocolate Cake

One-bowl recipes are lifesavers when you need to bake a party-pretty layer cake in record time. The only trick is to be sure to have the butter soft enough to blend easily into the batter.

PREP: 20 MINUTES PLUS COOLING   BAKE: 30 MINUTES
MAKES 12 SERVINGS

2 cups all-purpose flour
1 cup granulated sugar
3/4 cup packed brown sugar
2/3 cup unsweetened cocoa
1 1/2 teaspoons baking powder
1/2 teaspoon baking soda
1/2 teaspoon salt

1 1/2 cups milk
1/2 cup butter or margarine (1 stick), softened
2 large eggs
2 teaspoons vanilla extract
Peanut Butter Frosting (page 70)

1. Preheat oven to 350°F. Grease two 9-inch round cake pans.

2. In large bowl, combine flour, granulated and brown sugars, cocoa, baking powder, baking soda, salt, milk, butter, eggs, and vanilla. With mixer at low speed, beat until dry ingredients are moistened. Increase speed to high; beat until batter is smooth, about 3 minutes.

3. Divide batter equally between prepared pans. Bake until toothpick inserted in center comes out clean, about 30 minutes. Cool layers in pans on wire racks 10 minutes. Run thin knife around layers to loosen from sides of pans. Invert onto racks to cool completely.

4. Meanwhile, prepare Peanut Butter Frosting. Place one cake layer, rounded side down, on cake plate. With narrow metal spatula, spread 1/2 cup frosting over layer. Top with second layer, rounded side up. Spread remaining frosting over side and top of cake.

Each serving: About 550 calories, 9g protein, 72g carbohydrate, 27g total fat (13g saturated), 90mg cholesterol, 470mg sodium.

Chocolate Génoise with Ganache

Cakes don't get more elegant than a génoise covered with rich and creamy ganache. We recommend using a high-quality chocolate for the most decadent ganache.

PREP: 50 MINUTES PLUS COOLING   BAKE: 25 MINUTES
MAKES 20 SERVINGS

7 large eggs
1¹/₄ cups granulated sugar
1¹/₂ teaspoons vanilla extract
³/₄ cup cake flour (not self-rising)
³/₄ cup unsweetened cocoa

¹/₂ teaspoon salt
¹/₂ cup butter or margarine (1 stick),
  melted and cooled to lukewarm
Ganache (page 72)
confectioners' sugar

1. Preheat oven to 350°F. Grease two 9-inch round cake pans. Line bottoms with waxed paper; grease paper. Dust pans with cocoa.

2. In large bowl, with mixer at high speed, beat eggs, granulated sugar, and vanilla until mixture has increased in volume about four times and is the consistency of whipped cream. This will take 5 to 35 minutes.

3. Meanwhile, in medium bowl, combine flour, cocoa, and salt. Sift flour mixture one-fourth at a time, over egg mixture, and gently fold in.

4. Divide batter equally between prepared pans. Bake until cake springs back when lightly touched, about 25 minutes. Cool in pans on wire racks 10 minutes. Run thin knife around layers to loosen from sides of pans. Invert onto racks. Remove waxed paper; cool.

5. Meanwhile, prepare Ganache; let stand at room temperature 30 minutes.

6. With serrated knife, cut each cake layer horizontally in half. Place bottom half of one layer, cut side up, on cake plate. With narrow metal spatula spread with ¹/₃ cup ganache. Top with second layer, rounded side up, and spread with ¹/₃ cup ganache. Repeat layering to make 4 layers of cake and 3 layers of ganache in all. Dust cake with confectioners' sugar; spread remaining ganache on side of cake.

Each serving: About 260 calories, 4g protein, 29g carbohydrate, 16g total fat (9g saturated), 104mg cholesterol, 140mg sodium.

German's Chocolate Cake

Contrary to what most people think, this beloved chocolate cake is not a German creation. The correct name is German's, which was the brand name of an American baking chocolate from which it was first created.

PREP: 45 MINUTES PLUS COOLING   BAKE: 30 MINUTES
MAKES 16 SERVINGS

2 cups all-purpose flour	1 1/2 cups sugar
1 teaspoon baking soda	3/4 cup butter or margarine
1/4 teaspoon salt	(1 1/2 sticks), softened
1 1/4 cups buttermilk	4 squares (4 ounces) sweet baking
1 teaspoon vanilla extract	chocolate, melted
3 large eggs, separated	Coconut-Pecan Frosting (page 71)

1. Preheat oven to 350°F. Grease three 8-inch round cake pans. Line bottoms with waxed paper; grease paper. Dust pans with flour.

2. In small bowl, combine flour, baking soda, and salt. In measuring cup, mix buttermilk and vanilla.

3. In medium bowl, with mixer at medium-high speed, beat egg whites until frothy. Sprinkle in 3/4 cup sugar, 1 tablespoon at a time, beating until soft peaks form when beaters are lifted.

4. In large bowl, with mixer at medium speed, beat butter until light and fluffy. Add remaining 3/4 cup sugar and beat until well blended. Reduce speed to medium-low; add egg yolks, one at a time, beating well after each addition. Beat in melted chocolate. Reduce speed to low; add flour mixture alternately with buttermilk mixture, beginning and ending with flour mixture. Beat until smooth, occasionally scraping bowl. With rubber spatula, fold half of beaten egg whites into batter; gently fold in remaining egg whites.

5. Divide batter equally among prepared pans. Place two pans on upper oven rack and one pan on lower oven rack so pans are not directly above one another. Bake until toothpick inserted in center comes out almost clean, about 30 minutes. Cool in pans on wire racks 10 minutes. Run thin knife around layers to loosen from sides of pans. Invert onto racks. Remove waxed paper; cool completely.

6. Meanwhile, prepare Coconut-Pecan Frosting. Place one layer, rounded side down, on cake plate. With narrow metal spatula, spread 1 cup frosting over layer. Top with second cake layer, rounded side up, and spread with 1 cup frosting. Place remaining layer, rounded side up, on top. Spread remaining frosting over side and top of cake.

Each serving: About 505 calories, 5g protein, 53g carbohydrate, 31g total fat (16g saturated), 140mg cholesterol, 320mg sodium.

FROSTING LAYER CAKES

It is easiest to frost a cake if it is elevated and can be turned. If you don't have a cake decorating stand, place the cake on a serving plate set on a large coffee can or inverted bowl.

Brush off any crumbs and use a serrated knife to trim away any crisp edges. Place the first layer, rounded side down, on the serving plate. To keep the plate clean, tuck strips of waxed paper under the cake, covering the plate edge. Using a narrow metal spatula, spread one-half to two-thirds cup frosting on the cake layer top, spreading it almost to the edge. Top with the second cake layer, rounded side up. Thinly frost the cake to set the crumbs and keep them in place; first coat the top of the cake, then the side. Finish the cake with a thicker layer of frosting. Where the top and side of the frosting meet, smooth it by sweeping and swirling the edge of the frosting toward the center of the cake. Slip out the waxed paper strips and discard.

Checkerboard Cake

This cake is the best of both worlds: vanilla cake and chocolate cake rolled into one. Special checkerboard cake pans are available, but our easy, clever method uses standard round cake pans.

PREP: 40 MINUTES PLUS COOLING   BAKE: 25 MINUTES
MAKES 16 SERVINGS

3 1/2 cups cake flour (not self-rising)
1 tablespoon baking powder
1/2 teaspoon salt
1 cup butter or margarine (2 sticks), softened
2 cups sugar
1 1/4 cups milk

1 tablespoon vanilla extract
8 large egg whites
8 squares (8 ounces) semisweet chocolate, melted and cooled
Chocolate Buttercream Frosting (page 60)

1. Preheat oven to 350°F. Grease three 8-inch round cake pans. Line bottoms of cake pans with waxed paper; grease paper. Dust with flour.
2. In medium bowl, combine flour, baking powder, and salt.
3. In large bowl, with mixer at low speed, beat butter and 1 1/2 cups sugar until blended. Increase speed to high; beat until light and fluffy, about 5 minutes. Reduce speed to low. Add flour mixture, milk, and vanilla; beat until just combined. Increase speed to medium; beat 2 minutes, occasionally scraping bowl.
4. In separate large bowl, with mixer at high speed, beat egg whites until soft peaks form when beaters are lifted. Sprinkle in remaining 1/2 cup sugar, 2 tablespoons at a time, beating until sugar has dissolved and egg whites stand in stiff, glossy peaks when beaters are lifted. Do not overbeat. Gently fold beaten egg whites, one-third at a time, into flour mixture until blended. Spoon half of batter into medium bowl. Into batter remaining in large bowl, fold in melted chocolate until blended.
5. Spoon vanilla batter into large pastry bag with 1/2-inch opening (or use a heavy-duty plastic bag with corner cut to make 1/2-inch opening). Repeat with chocolate batter and separate large pastry bag with 1/2-inch opening. Pipe 1 1/2-inch-wide band of chocolate batter around inside edge of two cake pans. Pipe 1 1/2-inch-wide band of vanilla batter next to each chocolate band. Pipe in enough chocolate batter to fill center. In third

cake pan, repeat piping with alternating rings of batter, but starting with vanilla band around edge of pan.

6. Bake until toothpick inserted in center comes out clean, 25 to 30 minutes. Cool layers in pans on wire racks 10 minutes. Run thin knife around layers to loosen from sides of pans. Invert onto racks. Remove waxed paper; cool completely.

7. Meanwhile, prepare Chocolate Buttercream Frosting.

8. Place one of the two identical cake layers, rounded side down, on cake plate. With narrow metal spatula, spread 1/2 cup buttercream over layer. Top with reverse-design cake layer, rounded side up, and spread with 1/2 cup buttercream. Place remaining cake layer, rounded side up, on top. Spread remaining buttercream over side and top of cake.

Each serving: About 585 calories, 6g protein, 78g carbohydrate, 29g total fat (10g saturated), 34mg cholesterol, 459mg sodium.

Black Forest Cake

Our luscious three-layer chocolate extravaganza filled with cherries and kirsch-laced whipped cream celebrates two of Germany's glories: cherries from the Black Forest region and the potent brandy (kirsch) that is distilled from them.

PREP: 1 HOUR PLUS CHILLING BAKE: 25 MINUTES
MAKES 16 SERVINGS

CHOCOLATE CAKE
2 cups all-purpose flour
1 cup unsweetened cocoa
2 teaspoons baking powder
1 teaspoon baking soda
$1/2$ teaspoon salt
$1^1/3$ cups milk
2 teaspoons vanilla extract
1 cup butter or margarine (2 sticks), softened
2 cups sugar
4 large eggs

CHERRY FILLING
2 cans ($16^1/2$ ounces each) pitted dark sweet cherries (Bing) in heavy syrup
$1/3$ cup kirsch (cherry brandy)

CREAM FILLING
$1^1/2$ cups heavy or whipping cream
$1/2$ cup confectioners' sugar
2 tablespoons kirsch (cherry brandy)
1 teaspoon vanilla extract
Chocolate Curls (page 230)

1. Preheat oven to 350°F. Grease three 9-inch round cake pans. Line bottoms with waxed paper; grease paper. Dust pans with flour.

2. Prepare Chocolate Cake: In medium bowl, combine flour, cocoa, baking powder, baking soda, and salt. In measuring cup, mix milk and vanilla.

3. In large bowl, with mixer at low speed, beat butter and sugar until blended. Increase speed to high; beat until creamy, about 2 minutes. Reduce speed to medium-low; add eggs, one at a time, beating well after each addition. Add flour mixture alternately with milk mixture, beginning and ending with flour mixture, beating until batter is smooth, occasionally scraping bowl with rubber spatula.

4. Divide batter evenly among cake pans; spread evenly. Place two cake pans on upper oven rack and one on lower oven rack so pans are not directly above one another. Bake until toothpick inserted in center comes out almost clean, about 25 minutes. Cool in pans on wire racks 10 minutes. Run thin knife around layers to loosen from sides of pans. Invert onto racks. Remove waxed paper; cool completely.

5. Meanwhile, prepare Cherry Filling: Drain cherries well in sieve set over bowl. Reserve ½ cup syrup; stir in kirsch.

6. Prepare Cream Filling: In small bowl, with mixer at medium speed, beat cream, confectioners' sugar, kirsch, and vanilla until stiff peaks form.

7. Place one cake layer, rounded side down, on cake plate. Brush with one-third of syrup mixture. With narrow metal spatula, spread one-third of whipped-cream mixture over layer, top with half of cherries. Top with second cake layer, rounded side up. Brush with half of remaining syrup mixture, spread with half of remaining cream mixture, and top with remaining cherries. Place remaining layer, rounded side up, on top; brush with remaining syrup mixture. Spoon remaining cream mixture onto center of top layer, leaving a border.

8. Pile chocolate curls on top of whipped cream. Cover and refrigerate cake overnight.

Each serving: About 450 calories, 6g protein, 58g carbohydrate, 22g total fat (13g saturated), 118mg cholesterol, 344mg sodium.

Old-Fashioned Cocoa Cake

A sheet cake with a thick layer of chocolate buttercream—a great bring-along for a casual party.

Prep: 30 minutes plus cooling   Bake: 40 minutes
Makes 18 servings

2¹/₂ cups all-purpose flour

1¹/₂ cups sugar

³/₄ cup unsweetened cocoa

1¹/₂ teaspoons baking soda

³/₄ teaspoon salt

1¹/₂ cups buttermilk

³/₄ cup mayonnaise

1 tablespoon vanilla extract

2 large eggs

Rich Chocolate Frosting (page 59)

1. Preheat oven to 350°F. Grease 13" by 9" baking pan.

2. In large bowl, combine flour, sugar, cocoa, baking soda, and salt.

3. In medium bowl, with wire whisk, mix buttermilk, mayonnaise, vanilla, and eggs until almost smooth.

4. With wooden spoon, stir buttermilk mixture into flour mixture until smooth. Spoon into prepared baking pan. Bake until toothpick inserted in center comes out clean, 35 to 40 minutes. Cool cake in pan on wire rack.

5. Meanwhile, prepare Rich Chocolate Frosting. With narrow metal spatula, spread frosting over cake.

Each serving: About 385 calories, 5g protein, 52g carbohydrate, 20g total fat (4g saturated), 28mg cholesterol, 380mg sodium.

Rich Chocolate Cake

An extra-generous amount of unsweetened cocoa makes this cake the most chocolaty ever. We like it slathered with Fluffy White Frosting, but you can use any frosting you like.

PREP: 45 MINUTES PLUS COOLING   BAKE: 40 MINUTES
MAKES 20 SERVINGS

2 cups all-purpose flour
1 cup unsweetened cocoa
2 teaspoons baking powder
1 teaspoon baking soda
1/2 teaspoon salt
1 cup butter or margarine (2 sticks),
  softened

2 cups sugar
4 large eggs
2 teaspoons vanilla extract
1 1/3 cups milk
Fluffy White Frosting (page 69)

1. Preheat oven to 350°F. Grease 13" by 9" baking pan. Line bottom with waxed paper; grease paper. Dust pan with flour.
2. In bowl, combine flour, cocoa, baking powder, baking soda, and salt.
3. In large bowl, with mixer at low speed, beat butter and sugar until blended. Increase speed to high; beat until light and fluffy, about 5 minutes. Reduce speed to medium-low; add eggs, one at a time, beating well after each addition. Beat in vanilla. Mixture may appear grainy. Reduce speed to low; add flour mixture alternately with milk, beginning and ending with flour mixture. Beat until batter is smooth, occasionally scraping bowl with rubber spatula.
4. Pour batter into prepared pan. Bake until toothpick inserted in center comes out almost clean, 40 to 45 minutes. Cool in pan on wire rack 10 minutes. Run thin knife around cake to loosen from sides of pan. Invert onto rack. Remove waxed paper; cool completely.
5. Meanwhile, prepare Fluffy White Frosting. With narrow metal spatula, spread frosting over cake.

Each serving: About 285 calories, 4g protein, 43g carbohydrate, 12g total fat (7g saturated), 70mg cholesterol, 291mg sodium.

Warm Chocolate-Banana Cake

Chocolate lovers won't be deprived when they indulge in this lowfat rich-tasting brownielike cake with a fudgy texture. Serve with fat-free vanilla ice cream.

PREP: 15 MINUTES   BAKE: 35 MINUTES
MAKES 8 SERVINGS

1 cup all-purpose flour
1 cup unsweetened cocoa
1/2 cup granulated sugar
1 teaspoon baking powder
1/2 teaspoon salt
1/4 teaspoon ground cinnamon
1 ripe large banana, mashed
   (1/2 cup)

1 large egg, beaten
1/4 cup cold water plus 1 1/4 cups
   boiling water
2 tablespoons butter or margarine,
   melted
1 teaspoon vanilla extract
1/2 cup packed dark brown sugar

1. Preheat oven to 350°F. In large bowl, combine flour, 3/4 cup cocoa, granulated sugar, baking powder, salt, and cinnamon.

2. In medium bowl, with wooden spoon, stir banana, egg, cold water, butter, and vanilla until blended.

3. Stir banana mixture into flour mixture just until blended (batter will be thick). Spoon into ungreased 8-inch square baking dish; spread evenly.

4. In same large bowl, with wire whisk, beat brown sugar, remaining 1/4 cup cocoa, and boiling water until blended. Pour over chocolate batter in baking dish; do not stir.

5. Bake 35 minutes (dessert should have some fudgy sauce on top). Cool in pan on wire rack 5 minutes. Serve warm.

Each serving: About 235 calories, 5g protein, 47g carbohydrate, 5g total fat (3g saturated), 35mg cholesterol, 240mg sodium.

Flourless Chocolate-Walnut Cake

This cake is the perfect ending to a grand dinner. The cake can be prepared a few days ahead and stored, loosely covered, in the refrigerator. For the best flavor, let it come to room temperature before serving.

PREP: 30 MINUTES   BAKE: 50 MINUTES   MAKES 12 SERVINGS

3 squares (3 ounces) semisweet chocolate

3 squares (3 ounces) unsweetened chocolate

2 cups walnuts (8 ounces)

1 1/3 cups sugar

10 large eggs, separated

1/2 teaspoon salt

1 tablespoon confectioners' sugar (optional)

1. Preheat oven to 350°F. Grease 10" by 2 1/2" springform pan.

2. In 1-quart saucepan, melt semisweet and unsweetened chocolates over low heat, stirring occasionally, until smooth; cool.

3. In food processor with knife blade attached or in blender, combine walnuts and 1/3 cup sugar and process until very finely ground.

4. In large bowl, with mixer at high speed, beat egg yolks and 1/2 cup sugar until thick and lemon-colored, about 10 minutes, scraping bowl with rubber spatula. Fold in cooled melted chocolates. Wash and dry beaters.

5. In separate large bowl, with clean beaters and with mixer at high speed, beat egg whites and salt until soft peaks form when beaters are lifted. Sprinkle in remaining 1/2 cup sugar, 2 tablespoons at a time, beating until sugar has dissolved and egg whites stand in stiff, glossy peaks when beaters are lifted. Do not overbeat. With rubber spatula, fold nut mixture into chocolate mixture until blended (mixture will be thick). Gently fold in beaten egg whites, one-third at a time, just until blended.

6. Spoon batter into prepared springform pan; spread evenly. Bake until toothpick inserted in center comes out clean, about 50 minutes (do not overbake). Cool completely in pan on wire rack (cake may have some cracks on top). Run thin knife around cake to loosen from side of pan; remove pan side. Place cake on cake plate; sprinkle with confectioners' sugar just before serving.

Each serving: About 350 calories, 9g protein, 33g carbohydrate, 23g total fat (6g saturated), 177mg cholesterol, 155mg sodium.

Fabulous Flourless Chocolate Cake

This exceptionally sinful chocolate dessert is easy to make, but it must be refrigerated for twenty-four hours before serving for the best flavor and texture. For the neatest slices, dip the knife into hot water before cutting each one.

PREP: 1 HOUR PLUS OVERNIGHT TO CHILL   BAKE: 35 MINUTES
MAKES 20 SERVINGS

14 squares (14 ounces) semisweet chocolate, chopped
2 squares (2 ounces) unsweetened chocolate, chopped
1 cup butter (2 sticks; do not use margarine)

9 large eggs, separated
1/2 cup granulated sugar
1/4 teaspoon cream of tartar
confectioners' sugar

1. Preheat oven to 300°F. Remove bottom of 9" by 3" springform pan; cover with foil, wrapping foil around back. Replace pan bottom. Grease and flour foil bottom and side of pan.

2. In heavy 2-quart saucepan, melt semisweet and unsweetened chocolates and butter over low heat, stirring frequently, until smooth. Pour chocolate mixture into large bowl.

3. In small bowl, with mixer at high speed, beat egg yolks and granulated sugar until very thick and lemon-colored, about 10 minutes. With rubber spatula, stir egg-yolk mixture into chocolate mixture until blended. Wash and dry beaters.

4. In separate large bowl, with clean beaters and with mixer at high speed, beat egg whites and cream of tartar until soft peaks form when beaters are lifted. With rubber spatula, gently fold beaten egg whites, one-third at a time, into chocolate mixture just until blended.

5. Scrape batter into prepared pan; spread evenly. Bake 35 minutes. (Do not overbake; cake will firm upon standing and chilling.) Cool completely in pan on wire rack; refrigerate overnight in pan.

6. Run thin knife, rinsed under very hot water and dried, around cake to loosen from side of pan; remove side of pan. Invert onto cake plate; unwrap foil from pan bottom and lift off pan. Carefully peel foil away from cake.

7. To serve, let cake stand at room temperature 1 hour. Dust with confectioners' sugar. Or dust heavily with confectioners' sugar over paper doily or stencil.

Each serving: About 247 calories, 4g protein, 19g carbohydrate, 19g total fat (11g saturated), 120mg cholesterol, 125mg sodium.

Triple-Chocolate Fudge Cake

Dusting the cake pan with cocoa instead of flour avoids white streaks on the outside of the cake. If your cocoa has been sitting in your pantry for a while, press it through a strainer or sifter to remove any lumps.

PREP: 1 HOUR PLUS COOLING   BAKE 45 MINUTES
MAKES 16 SERVINGS

CAKE

1 cup all-purpose flour
1/3 cup unsweetened cocoa
1/2 teaspoon salt
8 squares (8 ounces) semisweet chocolate, chopped
1/2 cup butter or margarine (1 stick)
1 teaspoon instant-coffee powder or granules
1/4 cup hot water
6 large eggs, separated
1/4 teaspoon cream of tartar
1 cup sugar
1 1/2 teaspoons vanilla extract

CHOCOLATE GLAZE

1/2 cup semisweet chocolate chips
2 tablespoons butter or margarine
3 tablespoons milk
2 tablespoons light corn syrup

CHOCOLATE DRIZZLES

1 bar (1.55 ounces) milk chocolate
2 teaspoons vegetable shortening
2 ounces white chocolate

1. Preheat oven to 375°F. Grease 9" by 3" springform pan. Line bottom with waxed paper; grease paper. Dust with cocoa. Wrap outside of pan with heavy-duty foil.

2. In medium bowl, combine flour, cocoa, and salt. In small saucepan, melt semisweet chocolate and butter over low heat, stirring frequently until smooth. In cup, dissolve instant-coffee powder in hot water.

3. In small bowl, with mixer at high speed, beat egg whites and cream of tartar until soft peaks form when beaters are lifted. Sprinkle in 1/2 cup sugar, 2 tablespoons at a time, beating until sugar has dissolved and egg whites stand in stiff, glossy peaks when beaters are lifted. Do not overbeat.

4. In large bowl, with mixer at high speed, beat egg yolks and remaining 1/2 cup sugar until thick and lemon-colored, about 10 minutes. Reduce speed to low. Stir in flour mixture, chocolate mixture, coffee mixture, and vanilla until blended. With rubber spatula, gently fold in beaten egg whites. Pour batter into prepared pan.

5. Set springform pan in medium roasting pan. Fill roasting pan with enough boiling water to reach halfway up sides of pan. Bake the cake 45 minutes (center will still be slightly soft). Remove springform pan from roasting pan. Cool cake in springform pan on wire rack. Remove side of springform pan; invert cake onto cake plate. Remove waxed paper.

6. Prepare Chocolate Glaze: In 2-quart saucepan, melt chocolate chips and butter over low heat, stirring often until smooth. Remove from heat; stir in milk and corn syrup until blended. With narrow metal spatula, spread warm glaze over top of cooled cake, allowing it to run down side of cake.

7. Prepare Chocolate Drizzles: In 1-quart saucepan, melt milk chocolate and 1 teaspoon shortening over low heat, stirring often, until smooth. Spoon into small ziptight plastic bag. Wash and dry pan. In same clean pan, melt white chocolate and remaining 1 teaspoon shortening over low heat, stirring often, until smooth. Spoon white-chocolate mixture into separate small ziptight plastic bag. Cut very small hole in corner of each plastic bag. Drizzle milk and white chocolates over top of cake. Pull tip of knife or toothpick, through chocolates to make decorative design.

8. To serve, dip knife into hot water and dry immediately (the heated blade will cut through the cake without sticking). Cut cake into wedges.

Each serving: About 320 calories, 6g protein, 36g carbohydrate, 18g total fat (6g saturated), 81mg cholesterol, 205mg sodium.

Sacher Torte

This decadent Viennese chocolate dessert has two layers of apricot preserves and is covered with a chocolate glaze. Be traditional and serve the cake with *schlag* (whipped cream). And, of course, for the best results, we use butter, not margarine.

PREP: 45 MINUTES PLUS COOLING BAKE: 40 MINUTES
MAKES 10 SERVINGS

CAKE
3/4 cup butter (1 1/2 sticks), softened
   (do not use margarine)
3/4 cup confectioners' sugar
6 large eggs, separated
1 teaspoon vanilla extract
3 squares (3 ounces) unsweetened
   chocolate, chopped
3 squares (3 ounces) semisweet
   chocolate, chopped
1/4 teaspoon salt

1/4 teaspoon cream of tartar
1/2 cup granulated sugar
3/4 cup all-purpose flour
1 cup apricot preserves

CHOCOLATE GLAZE
3 squares (3 ounces) semisweet
   chocolate, chopped
2 tablespoons butter
1 teaspoon light corn syrup

1. Preheat oven to 350°F. Grease 9-inch springform pan. Line bottom of pan with waxed paper; grease paper. Dust pan with flour.

2. In large bowl, with mixer at medium speed, beat butter and confectioners' sugar until light and fluffy, about 3 minutes. Beat in egg yolks and vanilla until well blended.

3. In heavy 1-quart saucepan, melt unsweetened and semisweet chocolates over low heat, stirring frequently, until smooth. With mixer at medium speed, immediately beat melted chocolate into egg-yolk mixture until well blended. (Chocolate must be warm, about 130°F, when added to egg-yolk mixture, or batter will be too stiff.) Wash and dry beaters.

4. In medium bowl, with clean beaters and with mixer at high speed, beat egg whites, salt, and cream of tartar until soft peaks form when beaters are lifted. Sprinkle in granulated sugar, 2 tablespoons at a time, beating until sugar has dissolved and egg whites stand in stiff, glossy peaks when beaters are lifted. Do not overbeat. With rubber spatula, gently fold beaten egg whites, one-third at a time, into chocolate mixture, until blended. Sift flour, about 1/4 cup at a time, over chocolate mixture; gently fold in just until blended.

5. Scrape batter into prepared pan; spread evenly. Bake until toothpick inserted in center comes out clean, 40 to 45 minutes. Cool in pan on wire rack 10 minutes. Run thin knife around cake to loosen from side of pan; remove pan side. Invert cake onto rack. Slip knife under cake to separate from bottom of pan; remove pan bottom. Remove waxed paper; cool cake completely on rack.

6. When cake is cool, with serrated knife, cut horizontally into two layers. Place one layer, cut side up, on cake plate. In 1-quart saucepan, heat apricot preserves over medium-high heat until melted and bubbling. Strain through sieve set over small bowl. With pastry brush, brush half of preserves evenly over layer; replace top layer and spread evenly with remaining preserves. Let stand 10 minutes to set preserves slightly.

7. Prepare Chocolate Glaze: In heavy 1-quart saucepan, heat chocolate, butter, and corn syrup over low heat, stirring frequently, until chocolate and butter have melted and mixture is smooth. Remove from heat and cool slightly, about 5 minutes.

8. Pour chocolate glaze over cake. With narrow metal spatula, spread glaze, allowing some to drip down side of cake; completely cover top and side of cake. Let stand 30 minutes to allow glaze to set. If not serving right away, refrigerate up to 4 hours. Let cake stand 20 minutes at room temperature before serving.

Each serving: About 505 calories, 7g protein, 61g carbohydrate, 29g total fat (17g saturated), 171mg cholesterol, 276mg sodium.

Chocolate, Prune, and Nut Torte

The combination of chocolate, prunes, and pecans may seem unlikely, but they are a classic—and delicious—combination. Rich-tasting pecans work well here, but walnuts are also a good choice.

PREP: 1 HOUR PLUS OVERNIGHT TO CHILL   BAKE: 35 MINUTES
MAKES 12 SERVINGS

3 bittersweet chocolate bars
  (3 ounces each) or 9 squares
  (9 ounces) semisweet chocolate
6 large egg whites
1/2 cup granulated sugar
1/2 teaspoon vanilla extract

2 cups pitted prunes
  (about 10 ounces), diced
1 1/2 cups pecans (6 ounces), coarsely chopped
1 tablespoon confectioners' sugar

1. Grease 10" by 2 1/2" springform pan; line bottom of pan with waxed paper.

2. Finely grate chocolate. (Or, in food processor with knife blade attached, process chocolate until ground.)

3. Preheat oven to 425°F. In large bowl, with mixer at high speed, beat egg whites until soft peaks form when beaters are lifted. Sprinkle in granulated sugar, 2 tablespoons at a time, beating until sugar has dissolved and egg whites stand in stiff, glossy peaks when beaters are lifted. Beat in vanilla.

4. With rubber spatula, gently fold prunes and pecans into beaten egg whites; gently but thoroughly fold in grated chocolate. Pour into prepared pan; spread evenly. Bake until top of torte is deep brown and torte pulls away from side of pan, about 35 minutes.

5. Cool torte in pan on wire rack 15 minutes; remove side of pan. Invert torte and remove bottom of pan; remove waxed paper. Cool torte completely on rack. Cover and refrigerate overnight.

6. Just before serving, cut six 12" by 1/2" strips of waxed paper. Place strips, 1 inch apart, on top of torte. Dust torte with confectioners' sugar, then carefully lift off waxed-paper strips. Refrigerate any leftover torte.

Each serving: About 305 calories, 6g protein, 34g carbohydrate, 21g total fat (7g saturated), 0mg cholesterol, 30mg sodium.

Chocolate Pound Cake

Unlike some of the more extravagant chocolate creations, this tube cake sneaks up on you with its rich chocolate flavor. The coarsely grated chocolate, added last to the batter, is a unique accent. Use the large holes on the grater, so that you have small bits of chocolate rather than a fine powder.

PREP: 30 MINUTES PLUS COOLING   BAKE: 1 HOUR 20 MINUTES
MAKES 20 SERVINGS

3 cups all-purpose flour
1 cup unsweetened cocoa
1/2 teaspoon baking powder
11/2 cups butter or margarine
  (3 sticks), softened
23/4 cups sugar

2 teaspoons vanilla extract
5 large eggs
11/2 cups milk
2 ounces bittersweet or semisweet
  chocolate, grated

1. Preheat oven to 350°F. Grease and flour 10-inch tube pan with removable bottom. Line outside of pan with foil.

2. In medium bowl, combine flour, cocoa, and baking powder.

3. In large bowl, with mixer at medium speed, beat butter until creamy. Gradually add sugar, beating until fluffy, about 3 minutes. Beat in vanilla. Add eggs, one at a time, beating well after each addition, until blended. Reduce speed to low; beat in flour mixture alternately with milk, beginning and ending with flour mixture. Beat just until smooth, occasionally scraping bowl. Stir in grated chocolate.

4. Spoon batter into prepared pan; spread evenly. Bake until toothpick inserted in center comes out clean, 1 hour 20 to 25 minutes. Cool in pan on wire rack 10 minutes. Run thin knife around cake to loosen from side and center tube of pan; lift tube to separate cake from pan side. Slide knife under cake to separate from bottom of pan. Invert onto wire rack and remove center tube. Turn cake, right side up, onto rack to cool completely.

Each serving: About 360 calories, 5g protein, 47g carbohydrate, 18g total fat (10g saturated), 93mg cholesterol, 180mg sodium.

Chocolate Pound Cake with Irish Whiskey–Cream Sauce

This dense, decadent chocolate Bundt cake can also be served with a big dollop of vanilla- or rum-flavored whipped cream.

PREP: 30 MINUTES PLUS COOLING   BAKE: 1 HOUR 15 MINUTES
MAKES 20 SERVINGS

CHOCOLATE CAKE
3 cups all-purpose flour
1 cup unsweetened cocoa
1/2 teaspoon baking powder
1 1/2 cups butter or margarine
   (3 sticks), softened
2 3/4 cups sugar
2 teaspoons vanilla extract
5 large eggs
1 1/2 cups milk
2 ounces bittersweet chocolate or
   2 squares (2 ounces) semisweet
   chocolate, grated

IRISH WHISKEY–CREAM SAUCE
1 cup heavy or whipping cream
1/3 cup confectioners' sugar
1/4 cup freshly brewed coffee
2 tablespoons Irish whiskey or
   Bourbon

confectioners' sugar

1. Prepare Chocolate Cake: Preheat oven to 350°F. Grease and flour 12-cup Bundt pan. In medium bowl, combine flour, cocoa, and baking powder.

2. In large bowl, with mixer at medium speed, beat butter until creamy. Gradually beat in sugar, frequently scraping bowl with rubber spatula. Beat 3 minutes, occasionally scraping bowl. Beat in vanilla. Reduce speed to low; add eggs, one at a time, beating well after each addition. Add flour mixture alternately with milk, beginning and ending with flour mixture. Beat just until batter is blended, occasionally scraping bowl. Stir in grated chocolate.

3. Spoon batter into prepared pan; spread evenly. Bake until toothpick inserted in center of cake comes out clean, 1 hour 15 minutes. Cool cake in pan on wire rack 10 minutes. Invert cake onto wire rack to cool completely.

4. Meanwhile, prepare Irish Whiskey–Cream Sauce: In small bowl, with mixer at low speed, beat cream until frothy. Add sugar; increase speed to medium and beat until stiff peaks form. With rubber spatula or wire whisk, fold in coffee and whiskey until blended; cover and refrigerate up to 4 hours. Makes about 2 cups.

5. To serve, dust cake with confectioners' sugar. Cut cake into wedges and pass cream sauce to spoon over each serving.

Each serving without sauce: About 350 calories, 5g protein, 47g carbohydrate, 17g total fat (5g saturated), 93mg cholesterol, 177mg sodium.

Each tablespoon sauce: About 35 calories, 0g protein, 1g carbohydrate, 3g total fat (2g saturated), 10mg cholesterol, 5mg sodium.

Dusting Pan with Flour

Using a piece of folded paper towel or waxed paper, spread a thin layer of shortening inside the baking pan. Sprinkle about 1 tablespoon flour into the pan. Tilt to coat the bottom and side with the flour; invert the pan and tap out the excess flour.

Double-Chocolate Bundt Cake

This lowfat cake will satisfy a chocolate craving. If you use a dusting of confectioners' sugar instead of the glaze, you'll save thirty-five calories per slice.

PREP: 30 MINUTES PLUS COOLING   BAKE: 45 MINUTES
MAKES 20 SERVINGS

2¹/₄ cups all-purpose flour
1¹/₂ teaspoons baking soda
¹/₂ teaspoon baking powder
¹/₂ teaspoon salt
³/₄ cup unsweetened cocoa
1 teaspoon instant espresso-coffee powder
³/₄ cup hot water
2 cups sugar

¹/₃ cup vegetable oil
2 large egg whites
1 large egg
1 square (1 ounce) unsweetened chocolate, melted
2 teaspoons vanilla extract
¹/₂ cup buttermilk
Mocha Glaze (optional; page 73)

1. Preheat oven to 350°F. Generously spray 12-cup Bundt pan with nonstick cooking spray.

2. In medium bowl, combine flour, baking soda, baking powder, and salt.

3. In measuring cup, whisk cocoa and espresso-coffee powder into hot water until blended.

4. In large bowl, with mixer at low speed, beat sugar, oil, egg whites and egg until blended. Increase speed to high; beat until creamy, about 2 minutes. Reduce speed to low; beat in cocoa mixture, melted chocolate, and vanilla until blended. Add flour mixture alternately with buttermilk, beginning and ending with flour mixture. Beat just until blended, occasionally scraping bowl with rubber spatula.

5. Pour batter into prepared pan. Bake until toothpick inserted in center comes out clean, about 45 minutes. Cool cake in pan on wire rack 10 minutes. Run tip of knife around edge of cake to loosen from side of pan; invert onto rack to cool completely.

6. Prepare Mocha Glaze, if you like. Pour over cooled cake.

Each serving without glaze: About 185 calories, 3g protein, 34g carbohydrate, 5g total fat (1g saturated), 11mg cholesterol, 175mg sodium.

Each serving with glaze: About 220 calories, 3g protein, 43g carbohydrate, 5g total fat (1g saturated), 11mg cholesterol, 175mg sodium.

Triple Chocolate-Cherry Cake

You can make this delectable cake and stash it—well wrapped—in the freezer for up to one month. Then let it thaw, still in its wrapping, at room temperature.

PREP: 40 MINUTES PLUS COOLING BAKE: 1 HOUR 10 MINUTES
MAKES 16 SERVINGS

1³/₄ cups all-purpose flour
³/₄ unsweetened cocoa
1¹/₂ teaspoons baking soda
¹/₂ teaspoon salt
1 cup dried tart cherries
1 tablespoon instant espresso-coffee powder
1 tablespoon very hot water
1¹/₂ cups buttermilk
2 teaspoons vanilla extract

1 cup butter (2 sticks), softened (do not use margarine)
1³/₄ cups sugar
3 large eggs
2 squares (2 ounces) unsweetened chocolate, melted
1 package (6 ounces) semisweet-chocolate chips (1 cup)
confectioners' sugar
whipped cream (optional)

1. Preheat oven to 325°F. Grease and flour 10-inch Bundt pan.

2. In medium bowl, combine flour, cocoa, baking soda, and salt.

3. In small bowl, combine cherries with enough *very hot water* to cover; let stand at least 5 minutes to soften cherries. In measuring cup, dissolve espresso powder in very hot water; stir in buttermilk and vanilla.

4. In large bowl, with mixer at low speed, beat butter and sugar until blended, frequently scraping bowl with rubber spatula. Increase speed to medium; beat 2 minutes, occasionally scraping bowl. Reduce speed to low; add eggs, one at a time, beating well after each addition. At low speed, alternately add flour mixture and buttermilk mixture, beginning and ending with flour mixture; beat until smooth, occasionally scraping bowl.

5. Drain cherries and pat dry with paper towels. With rubber spatula, fold melted unsweetened chocolate into batter; fold in chocolate chips and drained cherries.

6. Pour batter into prepared pan. Bake until toothpick inserted in center comes out clean, 1 hour to 1 hour 10 minutes. Cool cake in pan on wire rack 10 minutes. Invert cake onto rack to cool completely.

7. To serve, dust confectioners' sugar over cake. Pass whipped cream separately, if you like.

Each serving without whipped cream: About 365 calories, 5g protein, 52g carbohydrate, 17g total fat (8g saturated), 72mg cholesterol, 345mg sodium.

Chocolate Angel Food Cake

Here's how to have your chocolate cake and eat it too—with virtually no fat! Using cocoa powder instead of solid chocolate, makes the magic possible. Serve the cake sprinkled with confectioners' sugar, if you like.

PREP: 30 MINUTES   BAKE: 35 TO 40 MINUTES
MAKES 12 SERVINGS

3/4 cup cake flour (not self-rising)	1 1/2 teaspoons cream of tartar
1/2 cup unsweetened cocoa	1/2 teaspoon salt
1 1/2 cups sugar	1 1/2 teaspoons vanilla extract
1 2/3 cups egg whites	
(12 to 14 large egg whites)	

1. Preheat oven to 375°F. Sift flour, cocoa, and 3/4 cup sugar through sieve set over medium bowl.

2. In large bowl, with mixer at medium speed, beat egg whites, cream of tartar, and salt until foamy. Increase speed to medium-high; beat until soft peaks form when beaters are lifted. Gradually sprinkle in remaining 3/4 cup sugar, 2 tablespoons at a time, beating until sugar has dissolved and egg whites stand in stiff, glossy peaks when beaters are lifted. Do not overbeat. Beat in vanilla.

3. Sift cocoa mixture, one-third at a time, over beaten egg whites; fold in with rubber spatula just until cocoa mixture is no longer visible. Do not overmix.

4. Scrape batter into ungreased 9- to 10-inch tube pan; spread evenly. Bake until cake springs back when lightly touched, 35 to 40 minutes. Invert cake in pan on metal funnel or bottle; cool completely in pan. Run thin knife around cake to loosen from side and center tube of pan. Remove from pan and place on cake plate.

Each serving: About 149 calories, 5g protein, 33g carbohydrate, 1g total fat (0g saturated), 0mg cholesterol, 155mg sodium.

Rich Chocolate Cupcakes

We've topped these cupcakes with our famous Fudge Frosting, but there are lots of other delicious possibilities in the Frostings section of this chapter. Or pipe on a generous whipped-cream rosette.

PREP: 15 MINUTES PLUS COOLING   BAKE: 22 MINUTES
MAKES 24 CUPCAKES

1^1/$_3$ cups all-purpose flour
^{2}/$_3$ cup unsweetened cocoa
1^1/$_2$ teaspoons baking powder
^{1}/$_2$ teaspoon baking soda
^{1}/$_2$ teaspoon salt
1 cup milk

1^1/$_2$ teaspoons vanilla extract
10 tablespoons butter or margarine
 (1^1/$_4$ sticks), softened
1^1/$_3$ cups sugar
2 large eggs
Fudge Frosting (page 62)

1. Preheat oven to 350°F. Line twenty-four 2^1/$_2$-inch muffin-pan cups with fluted paper liners.

2. In medium bowl, combine flour, cocoa, baking powder, baking soda, and salt. In measuring cup, mix milk and vanilla.

3. In large bowl, with mixer at low speed, beat butter and sugar just until blended. Increase speed to high; beat until mixture is light and creamy, about 3 minutes. Reduce speed to low; add eggs, one at a time, beating well after each addition. Add flour mixture alternately with milk mixture, beginning and ending with flour mixture. Beat just until combined, occasionally scraping bowl with rubber spatula.

4. Spoon batter into muffin-pan cups. Bake until toothpick inserted in center comes out clean, 22 to 25 minutes. Immediately remove cupcakes from pans and cool completely on wire rack.

5. Meanwhile, prepare Fudge Frosting; use to frost cupcakes.

Each cupcake without frosting: About 130 calories, 2g protein, 18g carbohydrate, 6g total fat (4g saturated), 33mg cholesterol, 160mg sodium.

Fallen Chocolate Soufflé Roll

A flourless confection with the texture and taste of a chocolate soufflé but without the worry of it collapsing! Unlike other jelly-roll cakes, this one is not rolled up while still hot. If any cracks appear after the cake is rolled, a generous dusting of confectioners' sugar will mask them.

PREP: 30 MINUTES PLUS COOLING AND CHILLING   BAKE: 15 MINUTES
MAKES: 16 SERVINGS

1 teaspoon instant espresso-coffee powder
3 tablespoons hot water
5 squares (5 ounces) semisweet chocolate
1 square (1 ounce) unsweetened chocolate
6 large eggs, separated
3/4 cup granulated sugar
1 teaspoon vanilla extract
3/4 teaspoon ground cinnamon
1/4 teaspoon salt
1/8 teaspoon ground cloves
1 1/2 cups heavy or whipping cream
1/4 cup coffee-flavored liqueur
5 tablespoons confectioners' sugar plus additional for dusting

1. Preheat oven to 350°F. Grease 15 1/2" by 10 1/2" jelly-roll pan. Line with waxed paper; grease paper. Dust pan with flour.

2. In cup, dissolve espresso powder in hot water. In top of double boiler set over simmering water, melt semisweet and unsweetened chocolates with espresso mixture, stirring frequently, until smooth.

3. In large bowl, with mixer at high speed, beat egg whites until soft peaks form when beaters are lifted. Sprinkle in 1/4 cup granulated sugar, 1 tablespoon at a time, beating until sugar has dissolved and egg whites stand in stiff, glossy peaks when beaters are lifted.

4. In small bowl, with mixer at high speed, beat egg yolks with remaining 1/2 cup granulated sugar until very thick and lemon-colored, about 10 minutes. Reduce speed to low; beat in vanilla, cinnamon, salt, and cloves. With rubber spatula, fold chocolate mixture into yolk mixture until blended. Gently fold one-third of beaten egg whites into chocolate mixture; fold chocolate mixture into remaining egg whites.

5. Scrape batter into prepared pan; spread evenly. Bake until firm to the touch, about 15 minutes. Cover cake with clean, damp kitchen towel; cool in pan on wire rack 30 minutes.

6. In large bowl, with mixer at medium speed, beat cream until soft peaks form. Beat in coffee liqueur and 3 tablespoons confectioners' sugar; beat until stiff peaks form.

7. Remove towel from cake; sift remaining 2 tablespoons confectioners' sugar over cake. Run thin knife around edges of cake to loosen from sides of pan. Cover cake with sheet of foil and a large cookie sheet; invert cake onto cookie sheet. Carefully remove waxed paper. With narrow metal spatula, spread whipped cream over cake, leaving 1/2-inch border. Starting from a long side and using foil to help lift cake, roll cake jelly-roll fashion (cake may crack). Place, seam side down, on long platter. Refrigerate at least 1 hour, or until ready to serve. Just before serving, dust with confectioners' sugar.

Each serving: About 215 calories, 4g protein, 21g carbohydrate, 14g total fat (8g saturated), 110mg cholesterol, 65mg sodium.

BEATING EGG WHITES

The bowl and beaters must be absolutely clean, because even the tiniest bit of fat will prevent peaks from forming. Stainless steel or glass bowls do the best job. For the fullest volume, use room-temperature egg whites.

To beat egg whites until "foamy" or "frothy," beat them until they form a mass of tiny clear bubbles. For "soft peaks," beat until the whites form soft rounded peaks that droop when the beaters are lifted. For "stiff glossy peaks," beat until the whites form peaks that hold their shape when the beaters are lifted but are still moist. Overbeaten whites look lumpy and watery—there is no way to salvage them. Simply begin again with new whites.

Molten Chocolate Cakes

When you cut into these warm cakes, their delectable molten centers flow out. You can assemble them up to twenty-four hours ahead and re-frigerate, or freeze up to two weeks. If you refrigerate the cakes, bake them for ten minutes; if they are frozen, bake for sixteen minutes. Serve with whipped cream or vanilla ice cream.

PREP: 20 MINUTES BAKE: 8 MINUTES
MAKES 8 SERVINGS

4 squares (4 ounces) semisweet chocolate, chopped
1/2 cup butter or margarine (1 stick), cut into pieces
1/4 cup heavy or whipping cream
1/2 teaspoon vanilla extract

1/4 cup all-purpose flour
1/4 cup sugar
2 large eggs
2 large egg yolks
whipped cream or vanilla ice cream (optional)

1. Preheat oven to 400°F. Grease eight 6-ounce custard cups. Dust with sugar.

2. In heavy 3-quart saucepan, combine chocolate, butter, and cream. Heat over low heat, stirring occasionally, until butter and chocolate have melted and mixture is smooth. Remove from heat. Add vanilla; with wire whisk, stir in flour just until mixture is smooth.

3. In medium bowl, with mixer at high speed, beat sugar, eggs, and egg yolks until thick and lemon-colored, about 10 minutes. Fold egg mixture, one-third at a time, into chocolate mixture until blended.

4. Divide batter equally among prepared custard cups. Place cups in jelly-roll pan for easier handling. Bake until edges of cakes are set but center still jiggles, 8 to 9 minutes. Cool in pan on wire rack 3 minutes. Run thin knife around cakes to loosen from sides of cups; invert onto dessert plates. Serve immediately with whipped cream or ice cream, if desired.

Each serving: About 281 calories, 4g protein, 20g carbohydrate, 22g total fat (12g saturated), 148mg cholesterol, 139mg sodium.

Silken Chocolate Cheesecake

Silken tofu adds a wonderful smooth texture to this lower-fat chocolate cheesecake. We dare you to stop at one forkful.

PREP: 25 MINUTES PLUS CHILLING   BAKE: 50 MINUTES
MAKES 12 SERVINGS

1 container (19 ounces) silken tofu
1 container (15 ounces) part-skim ricotta cheese
1 square (1 ounce) unsweetened chocolate
1 package (8 ounces) light cream cheese (Neufchâtel), softened

1 cup packed dark brown sugar
1/2 cup unsweetened cocoa
2 teaspoons vanilla extract
fresh strawberries (optional)

1. Preheat oven to 325°F. Line large sieve with two layers of paper towels and set over large bowl. Place tofu and ricotta in sieve and let stand 15 minutes to allow excess liquid to drain; discard liquid.

2. Transfer tofu mixture to food processor with knife blade attached; process until smooth. Remove 1/2 cup tofu mixture; set aside.

3. In 1-quart saucepan, melt chocolate over low heat, stirring frequently, until smooth. Add reserved tofu mixture to warm chocolate in pan; whisk until blended.

4. To tofu mixture remaining in food processor, add cream cheese, brown sugar, cocoa, vanilla, and chocolate mixture; process just until combined.

5. Pour mixture into 9" by 3" springform pan. Bake until chessecake is set 2 inches from edge but center still jiggles, about 50 minutes. Cool cheese-cake in pan on wire rack 1 hour. Cover loosely and refrigerate until well chilled, at least 6 hours or up to overnight.

6. To serve, remove side of pan; garnish with strawberries, if you like.

Each serving: About 205 calories, 9g protein, 25g carbohydrate, 9g total fat (5g saturated), 18mg cholesterol, 165mg sodium.

Chocolate Cheesecake

Calling all chocoholics! Here's a triple chocolate treat: chocolate wafers, semisweet chocolate, and cocoa.

PREP: 25 MINUTES PLUS COOLING AND CHILLING
BAKE: 1 HOUR PLUS STANDING
MAKES 16 SERVINGS

1 1/2 cups chocolate-wafer cookie crumbs (part of 9-ounce package)
3 tablespoons butter or margarine, melted
2 tablespoons plus 1 cup sugar
3 packages (8 ounces each) cream cheese, softened

1/4 cup unsweetened cocoa
4 large eggs
3/4 cup sour cream
1 1/2 teaspoons vanilla extract
8 squares (8 ounces) semisweet chocolate, melted and cooled

1. Preheat oven to 325°F. In 9" by 3" springform pan, combine cookie crumbs, melted butter, and 2 tablespoons sugar; stir with fork until evenly moistened. With hand, press mixture firmly onto bottom of pan. Bake 10 minutes. Cool completely in pan on wire rack.

2. In large bowl, with mixer at low speed, beat cream cheese until smooth. Beat in remaining 1 cup sugar and cocoa until blended, occasionally scraping bowl with rubber spatula. Reduce speed to low. Add eggs, one at a time, beating just until blended, scraping bowl. Beat in sour cream and vanilla. Add melted chocolate and beat until well blended.

3. Pour chocolate mixture over crust. Bake until cheesecake is set 2 inches from edge but center still jiggles, 50 to 55 minutes. Turn off oven; let cheesecake remain in oven with door ajar 1 hour. Remove from oven; run thin knife around edge of cheesecake to prevent cracking during cooling. Cool completely in pan on wire rack. Cover loosely and refrigerate until well chilled, at least 6 hours or up to overnight. Remove side of pan to serve.

Each serving: About 384 calories, 7g protein, 34g carbohydrate, 26g total fat (15g saturated), 111mg cholesterol, 237mg sodium.

FROSTINGS

Rich Chocolate Frosting

The combination of semisweet and unsweetened chocolates gives this frosting its perfect flavor balance.

PREP: 15 MINUTES   MAKES ABOUT 2 1/2 CUPS

4 squares (4 ounces) semisweet chocolate

2 squares (2 ounces) unsweetened chocolate

2 cups confectioners' sugar

3/4 cup butter or margarine (1 1/2 sticks), softened

1 teaspoon vanilla extract

1. In heavy 1-quart saucepan, melt semisweet and unsweetened chocolates over low heat, stirring frequently, until smooth. Remove from heat; cool to room temperature.

2. In large bowl, with mixer at low speed, beat confectioners' sugar, butter, and vanilla until almost combined. Add melted chocolates. Increase speed to high; beat until light and fluffy, about 1 minute.

Each tablespoon: About 75 calories, 0g protein, 8g carbohydrate, 6g total fat (3g saturated), 9mg cholesterol, 36mg sodium.

Chocolate Buttercream Frosting

PREP: 10 MINUTES   MAKES ABOUT 2 3/4 CUPS

2 cups confectioners' sugar
1 cup butter or margarine (2 sticks),
  softened
3 tablespoons milk

1 teaspoon vanilla extract
6 squares (6 ounces) semisweet
  chocolate, melted and cooled

In large bowl, with mixer at low speed, beat confectioner's sugar, butter, milk, vanilla, and cooled chocolate just until mixed. Increase speed to high; beat until light and fluffy, about 2 minutes, frequently scraping bowl with rubber spatula.

Each tablespoon: About 78 calories, 0g protein, 7g carbohydrate, 6g total fat (3g saturated), 3mg cholesterol, 51mg sodium.

Silky Chocolate Butter Frosting

This is our basic "silky" frosting in an intense chocolate mode. Cocoa replaces some of the flour, and there are 4 ounces of semisweet chocolate in the recipe, too.

PREP: 10 MINUTES PLUS COOLING COOK: 8 MINUTES
MAKES ABOUT 3 CUPS

3/4 cup sugar
1/4 cup all-purpose flour
3 tablespoons unsweetened cocoa
1 cup milk
1 cup butter or margarine (2 sticks),
  softened

1 tablespoon vanilla extract
4 squares (4 ounces) semisweet
  chocolate, melted and cooled

1. In 2-quart saucepan, combine sugar, flour, and cocoa. With wire whisk, gradually stir in milk until smooth. Cook over medium heat, stirring, until mixture thickens and boils. Reduce heat to low, cook, stirring constantly, 2 minutes. Remove from heat; cool completely.

2. In large bowl, with mixer at medium speed, beat butter until creamy. Gradually beat in cooled milk mixture, vanilla, and melted chocolate until blended and smooth.

Each tablespoon: About 65 calories, 0g protein, 6g carbohydrate, 5g total fat (3g saturated), 11mg cholesterol, 40mg sodium.

Fudge Frosting

An extra-generous amount of chocolate makes this a frosting that any true chocolate lover will appreciate.

PREP: 15 MINUTES   MAKES: ABOUT 2 CUPS

3 squares (3 ounces) semisweet chocolate

2 squares (2 ounces) unsweetened chocolate

1/2 cup butter or margarine (1 stick), softened

1 1/2 cups confectioners' sugar

1 1/2 teaspoons vanilla extract

2 to 3 tablespoons milk

1. In heavy 1-quart saucepan, melt semisweet and unsweetened chocolates over low heat, stirring frequently, until smooth. Remove from heat; cool slightly.

2. In large bowl, with mixer at low speed, beat melted chocolates and butter until blended. Add confectioners' sugar, vanilla, and 2 tablespoons milk; beat until smooth. Increase speed to medium-high; beat until frosting is light and fluffy, occasionally scraping bowl with rubber spatula. Beat in remaining 1 tablespoon milk as needed for easy spreading consistency.

Each tablespoon: About 75 calories, 1g protein, 8g carbohydrate, 5g total fat (3g saturated), 8mg cholesterol, 30mg sodium.

Milk-Chocolate Candy Bar Frosting

Subtle-tasting milk chocolate frosting is perfect for slathering over devil's food cake or our Checkerboard Cake (page 28).

PREP: 15 MINUTES   MAKES ABOUT 2 3/4 CUPS

3/4 cup butter (1 1/2 sticks), softened

3 milk-chocolate candy bars (1.55 ounces each), melted and cooled

1 1/2 cups confectioners' sugar

3 to 4 tablespoons milk

In large bowl, with mixer at low speed, beat softened butter and melted chocolate until blended. Add confectioners' sugar and 3 tablespoons milk. Beat until smooth, adding remaining 1 tablespoon milk as needed for easy spreading consistency. Increase speed to medium-high; beat until fluffy, about 1 minute.

Each tablespoon: About 70 calories, 0g protein, 6g carbohydrate, 5g total fat (3g saturated), 12mg cholesterol, 45mg sodium.

Semisweet Chocolate Frosting

The combination of semisweet and unsweetened chocolates prevents the frosting from becoming overly sweet.

PREP: 15 MINUTES   MAKES ABOUT 2 CUPS

4 squares (4 ounces) semisweet chocolate

1 square (1 ounce) unsweetened chocolate

1/2 cup butter (1 stick), softened

1 1/2 cups confectioners' sugar

1 1/2 teaspoons vanilla extract

3 to 4 tablespoons milk

1. In heavy 1-quart saucepan, melt semisweet and unsweetened chocolates over low heat, stirring frequently, until smooth. Cool slightly.

2. In large bowl, with mixer at low speed, beat melted chocolates and butter until blended. Add confectioners' sugar, vanilla, and 3 tablespoons milk; beat until smooth. Increase speed to medium–high; beat until light and fluffy, occasionally scraping bowl with rubber spatula. Beat in remaining 1 tablespoon milk as needed for easy spreading consistency.

Each tablespoon: About 70 calories, 0g protein, 8g carbohydrate, 5g total fat (4g saturated), 10mg cholesterol, 28mg sodium.

Malted-Milk Frosting

Prepare Semisweet Chocolate Frosting as directed but beat in **2 tablespoons malted-milk powder** with confectioners' sugar in Step 2. Coarsely chop **1/2 cup malted-milk ball candies;** sprinkle over frosted cake.

Each tablespoon: About 70 calories, 0g protein, 8g carbohydrate, 4g total fat (3g saturated), 10mg cholesterol, 28mg sodium.

Milk-Chocolate Frosting

Prepare Semisweet Chocolate Frosting as directed, but substitute **3 ounces milk chocolate,** melted and cooled, for semisweet chocolate.

Each tablespoon: About 65 calories, 0g protein, 8g carbohydrate, 4g total fat (3g saturated), 10mg cholesterol, 28mg sodium.

White Chocolate Buttercream Frosting

This scrumptious buttery, creamy frosting will make any cake—plain or fancy—very special.

PREP: 15 MINUTES   MAKES ABOUT 3 1/2 CUPS

1 cup butter (2 sticks), slightly softened
2 1/2 cups confectioners' sugar
6 ounces white chocolate, Swiss confectionary bars, or white baking bar, melted but still slightly warm
1/4 cup milk
1 1/2 teaspoons vanilla extract

In large bowl, with mixer at high speed, beat butter, confectioners' sugar, white chocolate, milk, and vanilla until just mixed. Increase speed to high; beat until light and fluffy, about 2 minutes.

Each tablespoon: About 67 calories, 0g protein, 7g carbohydrate, 4g total fat (3g saturated), 9mg cholesterol, 39mg sodium.

White Chocolate Butter Frosting

Use this luscious frosting on your favorite chocolate cake.

PREP: 15 MINUTES   MAKES ABOUT 3¹/2 CUPS

1 cup butter (2 sticks), softened (do
  not use margarine)
2 cups confectioners' sugar

6 ounces white chocolate, Swiss confectionery bars, or white baking
  bars, melted and cooled
3 tablespoons milk

In large bowl, with mixer at low speed, beat butter, confectioners' sugar, white chocolate, and milk just until combined. Increase speed to high; beat until light and fluffy, about 2 minutes, frequently scraping bowl with rubber spatula.

Each tablespoon: About 62 calories, 0g protein, 6g carbohydrate, 4g total fat (3g saturated), 9mg cholesterol, 37mg sodium.

Two-Tone
Brandied Butter Frosting

Just a touch of brandy (or cognac) adds elegance to this silky smooth frosting. If you like the combination of chocolate and fruit, substitute raspberry- or orange-flavored liqueur.

PREP: 15 MINUTES PLUS COOLING   COOK: 10 MINUTES
MAKES 1 1/2 CUPS OF EACH FLAVOR

1 cup sugar
1/2 cup all-purpose flour
1 cup milk
1 square (1 ounce) semisweet
   chocolate
1 square (1 ounce) unsweetened
   chocolate

1 cup butter or margarine (2 sticks),
   softened
2 tablespoons brandy
1 teaspoon vanilla extract

1. In 2-quart saucepan, combine sugar and flour. With wire whisk, mix in milk until smooth. Cook over medium-high heat, stirring often, until mixture thickens and boils. Reduce heat to low; cook, stirring constantly, 2 minutes. Remove from heat; cool completely.

2. Meanwhile, in heavy 1-quart saucepan, melt semisweet and unsweetened chocolates over low heat, stirring frequently, until smooth. Remove from heat; cool slightly.

3. In large bowl, with mixer at medium speed, beat butter until creamy. Gradually beat in cooled milk mixture. When mixture is smooth, beat in brandy and vanilla until blended. Spoon half of vanilla frosting into small bowl; stir cooled chocolate into remaining frosting in bowl.

Each tablespoon vanilla frosting: About 60 calories, 0g protein, 5g carbohydrate, 4g total fat (2g saturated), 11mg cholesterol, 40mg sodium.

Each tablespoon chocolate frosting: About 70 calories, 0g protein, 6g carbohydrate, 5g total fat (3g saturated), 11mg cholesterol, 40mg sodium.

Whipped Cream Frosting

For the times when a cake needs no more embellishment than some freshly whipped cream.

PREP: 5 MINUTES   MAKES ABOUT 4 CUPS

2 cups heavy or whipping cream   **1 teaspoon vanilla extract**
1/4 cup confectioners' sugar

In small bowl, with mixer at medium speed, beat cream, confectioners' sugar, and vanilla until stiff peaks form.

Each tablespoon: About 28 calories, 0g protein, 1g carbohydrate, 3g total fat (2g saturated), 10mg cholesterol, 3mg sodium.

Cocoa Whipped Cream Frosting

Prepare as directed but use **1/2 cup confectioners' sugar** and add **1/2 cup unsweetened cocoa.**

Each tablespoon: About 30 calories, 0g protein, 2g carbohydrate, 3g total fat (2g saturated), 10mg cholesterol, 3mg sodium.

Fluffy White Frosting

This irresistible marshmallowlike frosting is best enjoyed the day it is made. If you're planning on frosting a chocolate cake, omit the lemon juice.

PREP: 15 MINUTES   COOK: 7 MINUTES
MAKES ABOUT 3 CUPS

2 large egg whites
1 cup sugar
1/4 cup water
2 teaspoons fresh lemon juice
   (optional)

1 teaspoon light corn syrup
1/4 teaspoon cream of tartar

1. In medium bowl set over 3- to 4-quart saucepan filled with 1 inch simmering water (bowl should sit about 2 inches above water), with hand-held mixer at high speed, beat egg whites, sugar, water, lemon juice if using, corn syrup, and cream of tartar until soft peaks form when beaters are lifted and mixture reaches 160°F on candy thermometer, about 7 minutes.

2. Remove bowl from pan; beat egg-white mixture until stiff, glossy peaks form when beaters are lifted, 5 to 10 minutes longer.

Each tablespoon: About 17 calories, 0g protein, 4g carbohydrate, 0g total fat (0g saturated), 0mg cholesterol, 2mg sodium.

Peanut Butter Frosting

Here's how to make a dessert lover's dreams come true. Serve up Cocoa Brownies (page 114) or One-Bowl Chocolate Cake (page 24) lavished with this creamy frosting.

PREP: 10 MINUTES   MAKES ABOUT 2 3/4 CUPS

1/2 cup butter or margarine (1 stick), softened
1/2 cup creamy peanut butter
1 package (3 ounces) cream cheese, softened

1 teaspoon vanilla extract
2 cups confectioners' sugar
2 to 3 tablespoons milk

1. In large bowl, with mixer at medium speed, beat butter, peanut butter, cream cheese, and vanilla until smooth and fluffy.

2. Add confectioners' sugar and 2 tablespoons milk; beat until blended. Increase speed to medium–high; beat until fluffy, about 2 minutes, adding remaining 1 tablespoon milk as needed for desired spreading consistency.

Each tablespoon: About 65 calories, 1g protein, 6g carbohydrate, 4g total fat (2g saturated), 8mg cholesterol, 40mg sodium.

Coconut-Pecan Frosting

This unique cooked frosting is an absolute must for German's Chocolate Cake (page 26); you can also spread it on any chocolate or vanilla layer or sheet cake.

PREP: 5 MINUTES   COOK: 15 MINUTES
MAKES ABOUT 3 CUPS

1/2 cup butter or margarine (1 stick), cut into pieces
1 cup heavy or whipping cream
1 cup packed light brown sugar
3 large egg yolks
1 teaspoon vanilla extract
1 cup flaked sweetened coconut
1 cup pecans (4 ounces), chopped

1. In 2-quart saucepan, combine butter, cream, and brown sugar. Heat almost to boiling over medium-high heat, stirring occasionally.

2. Place egg yolks in medium bowl. Slowly pour about 1/2 cup hot sugar mixture into egg yolks, whisking constantly. Reduce heat to medium-low. Add egg-yolk mixture to saucepan; whisk until mixture has thickened (do not boil). Remove from heat. Stir in vanilla, coconut, and pecans until combined. Cool to room temperature.

Each tablespoon: About 80 calories, 1g protein, 6g carbohydrate, 6g total fat (3g saturated), 25mg cholesterol, 30mg sodium.

Ganache

Ganache is a thick, creamy chocolate filling meant to be slathered between layers of your favorite cake.

PREP: 15 MINUTES PLUS CHILLING   MAKES 2 CUPS

1 cup heavy or whipping cream
2 tablespoons sugar
2 teaspoons butter or margarine
10 squares (10 ounces) semisweet
  chocolate, chopped

1 teaspoon vanilla extract
1 to 2 tablespoons brandy or orange-
  or almond-flavored liqueur
  (optional)

1. In 2-quart saucepan, combine cream, sugar, and butter; heat to boiling over medium-high heat. Remove from heat.

2. Add chocolate to cream mixture; with wire whisk stir until chocolate melts and mixture is smooth. Stir in vanilla and brandy, if using. Pour into jelly-roll pan and refrigerate until spreadable, at least 30 minutes.

Each tablespoon: About 74 calories, 1g protein, 6g carbohydrate, 6g total fat (3g saturated), 11mg cholesterol, 6mg sodium.

Chocolate Glaze

Pour or spread the warm (not hot) glaze over Éclairs (page 210). The glaze will thicken and set as it cools.

PREP: 5 MINUTES   COOK: 3 MINUTES   MAKES ABOUT $^1/_2$ CUP

3 squares (3 ounces) semisweet
  chocolate, coarsely chopped
3 tablespoons butter

1 tablespoon light corn syrup
1 tablespoon milk

In heavy 1-quart saucepan, heat chocolate, butter, corn syrup, and milk over low heat, stirring occasionally, until smooth.

Each tablespoon: About 100 calories, 1g protein, 9g carbohydrate, 8g total fat (5g saturated), 12mg cholesterol, 50mg sodium.

Mocha Glaze

PREP: 5 MINUTES   MAKES ABOUT 1 CUP

$^1/_4$ teaspoon instant espresso-coffee
  powder
2 tablespoons hot water
3 tablespoons unsweetened cocoa

3 tablespoons dark corn syrup
1 tablespoon coffee-flavored liqueur
1 cup confectioners' sugar

In medium bowl, dissolve coffee powder in hot water. Stir in cocoa, corn syrup, and liqueur until blended. Stir in confectioners' sugar until smooth.

Each tablespoon: About 45 calories, 0g protein, 11g carbohydrate, 0g total fat (0g saturated), 0mg cholesterol, 5mg sodium.

BREADS

Chocolate-Walnut Coffee Cake Wreath

A yeast cake that will fit nicely on your holiday buffet table. You can make this ahead—wrap well and freeze up to one month.

PREP: 40 MINUTES PLUS RISING AND COOLING   BAKE: 30 MINUTES
MAKES 1 COFFEE CAKE, ABOUT 16 SLICES

COFFEE CAKE
1/2 cup warm water (105° to 115°F)
2 packages active dry yeast
1 teaspoon plus 1/2 cup granulated
  sugar
1/2 cup butter or margarine (1 stick),
  softened
1 large egg
1/2 teaspoon salt
about 3 1/4 cups all-purpose flour

CHOCOLATE-WALNUT FILLING
3 squares (3 ounces) semisweet
  chocolate, chopped
1 square (1 ounce) unsweetened
  chocolate, chopped
3/4 cup low-fat sweetened condensed
  milk
1 cup walnuts (4 ounces), toasted
  (page 97) and chopped

ICING
1 cup confectioners' sugar
2 tablespoons milk

1. Prepare Coffee Cake: In cup, combine warm water, yeast, and 1 teaspoon granulated sugar; stir to dissolve. Let stand until foamy, about 5 minutes.

2. Meanwhile, in large bowl, with mixer at low speed, beat butter and remaining 1/2 cup granulated sugar until blended. Increase speed to high; beat until light and fluffy, about 2 minutes, occasionally scraping bowl with rubber spatula. Reduce speed to low; beat in egg until blended. Beat in yeast mixture, salt, and 1/2 cup flour (batter will look curdled) just until blended. With wooden spoon, stir in 2 1/2 cups flour until blended.

3. Turn dough onto lightly floured surface and knead until smooth and elastic, about 8 minutes, working in enough of remaining 1/4 cup flour just to keep dough from sticking. Shape dough into ball; place in greased large bowl, turning dough over to grease top. Cover bowl with plastic wrap and let rise in warm place (80° to 85°F) until doubled in volume, about 1 hour.

4. Meanwhile, prepare Chocolate-Walnut Filling: In 1-quart saucepan, heat semisweet and unsweetened chocolates and condensed milk over low heat, stirring occasionally, until chocolate has melted and mixture is smooth. Remove from heat. Cool filling to room temperature. Stir in walnuts. Cover and refrigerate until ready to use.

5. Punch down dough. Turn dough onto lightly floured surface; cover and let rest 15 minutes. Meanwhile, grease large cookie sheet.

6. With floured rolling pin, roll dough into 18" by 12" rectangle. Spread filling over dough to within 1/2 inch of edges. Starting at a long side, roll up dough jelly-roll fashion. Carefully lift roll and place, seam side down, on prepared cookie sheet. Shape roll into ring; press ends together to seal. With knife or kitchen shears, cut ring at 1 1/2-inch intervals, up to, but not completely through, inside dough edge. Gently pull and twist each cut piece to show filling. Dough will be soft, so use small metal spatula to help lift pieces. Cover and let rise in warm place until slightly risen, about 1 hour.

7. Meanwhile, preheat oven to 350°F. Bake coffee cake until golden, 30 to 35 minutes. Transfer to wire rack to cool.

8. Prepare Icing: In small bowl, mix confectioners' sugar with milk until smooth. When coffee cake is cool, drizzle with icing.

Each slice: About 335 calories, 6g protein, 47g carbohydrate, 15g total fat (6g saturated), 32mg cholesterol, 155mg sodium.

Chocolate-Cherry Bread

A not-too-sweet bread studded with bits of bittersweet chocolate and dried tart cherries. We use Dutch-process cocoa instead of the more usual natural cocoa to give the bread a richer brown color.

PREP: 20 MINUTES PLUS RISING   BAKE: 20 MINUTES
MAKES 2 LOAVES, 12 SLICES EACH

$1/4$ cup warm water (105° to 115°F)
1 package active dry yeast
3 teaspoons granulated sugar
about 3 $1/2$ cups all-purpose flour
$1/3$ cup unsweetened Dutch-process cocoa
$1/3$ cup packed brown sugar
1 $3/4$ teaspoons salt
1 cup freshly brewed coffee, cooled until warm (105° to 115°F)

4 tablespoons butter or margarine, softened
1 large egg, separated
$3/4$ cup dried tart cherries
3 squares (3 ounces) bittersweet chocolate, coarsely chopped
1 teaspoon water

1. In cup, combine warm water, yeast, and 1 teaspoon granulated sugar; stir to dissolve. Let stand until foamy, about 5 minutes.

2. Meanwhile, in large bowl, combine 3 cups flour, cocoa, brown sugar, and salt.

3. With wooden spoon, stir warm coffee, butter, egg yolk (cover egg white and set aside in refrigerator), and yeast mixture into flour mixture. In bowl, with floured hands, knead several times to combine well.

4. Turn dough onto lightly floured surface and knead until smooth and elastic, about 10 minutes, working in enough of remaining $1/2$ cup flour just to keep dough from sticking. Knead in cherries and chocolate.

5. Shape dough into ball; place in greased large bowl, turning dough to grease top. Cover bowl with plastic wrap and let rise in warm place (80° to 85°F) until doubled in volume, about 1 hour 30 minutes.

6. Punch down dough. Turn dough onto lightly floured surface and cut in half; cover dough and let rest 15 minutes for easier shaping.

7. Shape each dough half into 5-inch ball. Using the sides of your hands, tuck sides of dough under to meet in center. Rotate and repeat to form taut ball. Place balls, 3 inches apart, in opposite corners of ungreased large cookie sheet. Cover and let rise in warm place until doubled, about 1 hour.

8. Preheat oven to 400°F. In cup, beat reserved egg white with water; use to brush tops of loaves. Sprinkle loaves with remaining 2 teaspoons granulated sugar. With serrated knife or single-edge razor blade, cut shallow X in top of each loaf. Bake until loaves are crusty, about 20 minutes. Transfer to wire racks to cool.

Each slice: About 137 calories, 3g protein, 24g carbohydrate, 4g total fat (2g saturated), 14mg cholesterol, 202mg sodium.

KNEADING DOUGH

Knead in just enough flour to prevent the dough from sticking to the work surface (too much flour makes a dry, heavy loaf). Doughs that are sweet and rich or contain wholegrain flours should be somewhat sticky.

Place the dough on a lightly floured surface. To knead, fold about one-fourth of the dough onto the top of the dough mass, then push it down and away from you with the heel of your hand. Give the dough a quarter turn. Repeat until the dough is smooth and elastic and tiny blisters appear on the surface. This will usually take from eight to ten minutes.

Chocolate Swirl Almond Cake

Almond paste adds moistness and rich almond flavor to this delicious tea cake. To keep unused almond paste so it doesn't dry out, wrap it in a double thickness of plastic and pop it into a plastic bag and store at room temperature. Don't forget to remove all the air from the bag.

PREP: 15 MINUTES   BAKE: 1 HOUR
MAKES 1 LOAF, 16 SLICES

1³/4 cups all-purpose flour
2 teaspoons baking powder
1/4 teaspoon salt
1 cup sugar
4 ounces almond paste (about half 7- to 8-ounce can or tube), cut into pieces

1/2 cup butter or margarine (1 stick), softened
2/3 cup milk
2 large eggs
1 teaspoon vanilla extract
3 squares (3 ounces) semisweet or 3 ounces bittersweet chocolate, melted and cooled

1. Preheat oven to 350°F. Grease 9" by 5" metal loaf pan; dust with flour. In medium bowl, combine flour, baking powder, and salt; set aside.

2. In food processor with knife blade attached, combine sugar and almond paste; pulse until fine crumbs form. Add butter; process 1 minute, occasionally scraping bowl.

3. Add flour mixture, milk, eggs, and vanilla; pulse until well blended, occasionally scraping bowl.

4. Spread one-third of batter (about 1¼ cups) in prepared pan. Drizzle top with half of melted chocolate. Repeat with half of batter and remaining chocolate. Top with remaining batter.

5. Bake until toothpick inserted in center of loaf comes out clean, 1 hour to 1 hour 5 minutes.

6. Cool loaf in pan on wire rack 10 minutes. With small metal spatula or thin knife, loosen cake from sides of pan. Unmold and cool completely.

Each serving: About 225 calories, 4g protein, 30g carbohydrate, 11g total fat (5g saturated), 44mg cholesterol, 170mg sodium.

Chocolate-Cherry Coffee Cake

Three layers of a rich sour cream batter and two layers of a warmly spiced cocoa and chocolate chip crumb mixture make our coffee cake special. Unlike yeast-based coffee cakes, this one will stay nice and moist for several days. Enjoy it with a mid-morning cup of coffee or lightly toasted and spread with cream cheese for breakfast.

PREP: 30 MINUTES PLUS COOLING   BAKE: 1 HOUR 10 MINUTES
MAKES 16 SERVINGS

1/2 cup semisweet-chocolate
  mini-chips
1 2/3 cups sugar
1 tablespoon unsweetened cocoa
2 teaspoons ground cinnamon
3 cups all-purpose flour
1 1/2 teaspoons baking powder
1/2 teaspoon salt

3/4 cup butter or margarine
  (1 1/2 sticks), softened
1 container (16 ounces) light
  sour cream
3 large eggs
2 teaspoons vanilla extract
2/3 cup dried tart cherries
confectioners' sugar

1. Preheat oven to 350°F. Grease and flour 10-inch Bundt pan. In small bowl, combine chocolate mini-chips, 1/3 cup sugar, cocoa, and cinnamon. In another small bowl, combine flour, baking powder, and salt.

2. In large bowl, with mixer at low speed, beat butter and remaining 1 1/3 cups sugar until blended. Increase speed to medium; beat until light and creamy, about 2 minutes, occasionally scraping bowl with rubber spatula. Reduce speed to low. Add flour mixture, sour cream, eggs, and vanilla; beat until well mixed. Increase speed to medium; beat 2 minutes, occasionally scraping bowl. Stir in dried cherries.

3. Spread one-third of batter in prepared pan; sprinkle with half of chocolate mixture. Top with half of remaining batter; sprinkle with remaining chocolate mixture. Spread remaining batter on top.

4. Bake until toothpick inserted halfway between side and center tube comes out clean, about 1 hour 10 minutes. Cool cake in pan on wire rack 10 minutes. Invert cake onto rack to cool completely. To serve, dust cake with confectioners' sugar.

Each serving: About 345 calories, 5g protein, 50g carbohydrate, 14g total fat (7g saturated), 72mg cholesterol, 333mg sodium.

Chocolate Tea Bread

This rich and chocolaty tea bread makes the most special tea time or breakfast treat. Serve it with whipped cream cheese and raspberry jam. What a great way to begin the day.

PREP: 15 MINUTES   BAKE: 1 HOUR
MAKES 1 LOAF, 16 SLICES

1¾ cups all-purpose flour
¾ cup unsweetened cocoa
½ teaspoon baking soda
½ teaspoon salt
½ cup butter or margarine (1 stick), softened

1¼ cups sugar
2 large eggs
1 teaspoon instant espresso-coffee powder
1 teaspoon vanilla extract
1 container (8 ounces) sour cream

1. Preheat oven to 350°F. Grease 9" by 5" metal loaf pan; dust with cocoa. In medium bowl, combine flour, cocoa, baking soda, and salt.

2. In large bowl, with mixer at medium-high speed, beat butter until creamy. Gradually add sugar; beat until well blended. Reduce speed to low; add eggs, one at a time, beating well after each addition until well blended, occasionally scraping bowl with rubber spatula. Beat in espresso powder and vanilla. Add flour mixture alternately with sour cream, beginning and ending with flour mixture; beat just until blended. Spoon batter into prepared pan.

3. Bake until toothpick inserted in center of loaf comes out clean, 1 hour to 1 hour 5 minutes. Cool in pan on wire rack 10 minutes; remove loaf from pan and cool completely.

Each serving: About 213 calories, 3g protein, 29g carbohydrate, 10g total fat (6g saturated), 48mg cholesterol, 187mg sodium.

Chocolate Waffles

The only thing better than waffles is chocolate waffles. Serve them for dessert with hot fudge sauce or for brunch, accompanied by bowls of sliced strawberries and bananas, your favorite granola, and plain whole-milk yogurt flavored with pure vanilla extract and a touch of sugar.

PREP: 10 MINUTES   BAKE: 3 MINUTES PER BATCH
MAKES EIGHT 4" BY 4" WAFFLES OR 8 SERVINGS

6 tablespoons butter or margarine, cut into pieces
3 squares (3 ounces) unsweetened chocolate, coarsely chopped
1 cup all-purpose flour
1½ teaspoons baking powder
¼ teaspoon salt

¾ cup sugar
3 large eggs
⅓ cup cold brewed coffee
1 teaspoon vanilla extract
vanilla ice cream
hot fudge sauce (such as our Hot Fudge Sauce, page 229)

1. In small microwave-safe bowl, combine butter and chocolate. Cover with plastic wrap, turning back one section to vent. Microwave on High 1 minute; stir until smooth. Cool.

2. Preheat waffle baker as manufacturer directs. In large bowl, combine flour, baking powder, and salt. In medium bowl, mix sugar, eggs, coffee, and vanilla; whisk in cooled chocolate mixture until blended. Add chocolate mixture to flour mixture; whisking until smooth.

3. When waffle baker is ready, pour batter into center; spread to within 1 inch of edges. Cover and bake 3 minutes; do not lift cover during baking. (Waffle will not be crisp. Do not overcook; batter burns easily.)

4. When waffle is done, lift cover and loosen waffle with fork. Serve immediately with ice cream and hot fudge sauce, or keep warm in oven (place waffle directly on oven rack). Reheat waffle baker before pouring in more batter.

Each serving: About 291 calories, 5g protein, 34g carbohydrate, 16g total fat (9g saturated), 103mg cholesterol, 277mg sodium.

Chocolate Panini

Panini, Italian for "small sandwiches," are a part of everyday life in Italy that has been embraced here. For this version, a piece of chocolate and a dollop of chocolate-hazelnut spread are sandwiched between slices of rich egg bread. We used challah, but brioche is also a good choice. The sandwiches are grilled until the bread is golden and grill marked and the chocolate melty and fabulous.

PREP: 10 MINUTES   BAKE: 2 MINUTES
MAKES 4 SERVINGS

4 (6 1/2" x 4" x 1/2") slices challah or
   other egg bread
2 tablespoons butter, softened

2 tablespoons chocolate-hazelnut
   spread (optional)
1 bar (4 ounces) bittersweet or semisweet chocolate, cut in half

1. Preheat panini baker or waffle maker as manufacturer directs.

2. Spread one side of each bread slice with butter. Arrange 2 slices, buttered side down, on sheet of waxed paper; spread each slice with 1 tablespoon chocolate hazelnut spread, if using. Top each slice with 1 piece chocolate. Cover with remaining slices, buttered side up.

3. When panini baker is ready, add sandwiches. (If panini baker is not large enough, bake 1 panini at a time.) Cover and bake 2 minutes; do not lift cover during baking. When panini are golden, lift cover and transfer to cutting board. Cut each panini in half.

Each serving: About 333 calories, 7g protein, 40g carbohydrate, 19g total fat (10g saturated), 41mg cholesterol, 305mg sodium.

PIES & TARTS

Pies and tarts are close cousins: they each have a crust and a filling. The main difference is that a pie is casual, homey, and made in a slope-sided pie plate from which it is also served. A tart is a little fancier. It is made in a straight-sided pan that has fluted sides and a removable bottom. A tart is always transferred from its pan to a serving plate. In this chapter all of our luscious pies and tarts have one thing in common: they're all fabulous because they're made with chocolate. Here you will find our favorite Chocolate Cream Pie as well as a decadent Chocolate-Caramel Walnut Tart and an easy No-Bake Chocolate Fudge Tart. Just follow our tips to make these desserts . . . as easy as pie.

Doughs and Don'ts

A pie or tart is only as good as its crust, so here's how to bake the best.

The flavor and texture of a crust depends on its main ingredients: flour and fat. Butter gives dough flavor, crispness, and color; vegetable shortening makes it flaky. We like to use a combination of butter and shortening.

Mix It Right A pastry blender is the best tool for blending fat and flour. Work quickly so the fat remains firm. Sprinkle in the water, 1 tablespoon at a time, tossing with a fork after each addition. When enough water has been added, the dough will no longer look dusty. Shape it into one or more disks. Wrap in plastic and chill for at least 30 minutes, so it has a chance to firm up and the water can distribute itself throughout the dough.

Roll It Out Lightly dust the surface (and rolling pin) with flour. To roll the dough into a round, start in the center and roll up to the edge. Give the dough a quarter turn; repeat rolling and rotating until you have a round.

A Perfect Fit We like to use glass or dull metal pie plates. To transfer dough to a pie plate or tart pan; loosely roll the dough onto the rolling pin. Position the pin at one side of the pie plate and unroll the dough. Or fold the dough into quarters, set it into the pan and unfold. Gently press the dough against the bottom and side of the pan (do not stretch it).

Make It Pretty You can use your fingertips to crimp and shape a rope or scalloped edge, use a fork to make an old-fashioned forked edge, or use a knife to make slits around the edge at about 1/4-inch intervals and fold over every other piece to form a turret edge. If you have more time, use an aspic cutter to cut out decorative shapes, such as hearts or leaves, and attach them to the plain edge with water or beaten egg white.

Chocolate-Cream Angel Pie

This time-tested favorite is made with whipped chocolate cream nestled in a meringue crust. Heavenly!

Prep: 30 minutes plus cooling   Bake: 1 hour
Makes 10 servings

3 large egg whites
1/4 teaspoon cream of tartar
1/4 teaspoon salt
2 1/4 cups confectioners' sugar
2 1/2 teaspoons vanilla extract
1/2 cup unsweetened cocoa

1 teaspoon instant espresso-coffee powder
1 teaspoon hot water
2 tablespoons milk
2 cups heavy or whipping cream
Chocolate Curls (page 230)

1. Preheat oven to 300°F. Line 9-inch pie plate with foil, extending foil over rim of plate. Press foil against pie plate; grease and flour foil.

2. In small bowl, with mixer at high speed, beat egg whites, cream of tartar, and salt until soft peaks form when beaters are lifted. Sprinkle in 1 cup confectioners' sugar, 2 tablespoons at a time, beating until sugar has dissolved. Add 1 teaspoon vanilla; continue beating until egg whites stand in stiff, glossy peaks when beaters are lifted.

3. With large spoon, spread meringue evenly over bottom and up side of pie plate, extending meringue 1/2 inch above rim of pie plate. Bake 1 hour. Turn off oven and let meringue remain in oven 1 hour to dry. Cool meringue shell completely in pie plate on wire rack. Lift shell from pie plate and peel off foil. Place shell on serving plate.

4. Meanwhile, prepare filling: Sift cocoa with remaining 1 1/4 cups confectioners' sugar. In cup, dissolve espresso powder in hot water; stir in milk. In large bowl, with mixer at medium speed, beat cream, espresso, and remaining 1 1/2 teaspoons vanilla until soft peaks form. Reduce speed to low; gradually beat in cocoa mixture until thoroughly blended and stiff peaks form.

5. With rubber spatula, spread chocolate cream in cooled meringue shell. If not serving right away, cover pie and refrigerate until ready to serve, up to 4 hours. Sprinkle with chocolate curls.

Each serving: About 289 calories, 3g protein, 31g carbohydrate, 18g total fat (11g saturated), 66mg cholesterol, 95mg sodium.

Chocolate Cream Pie

Cream pies, as we know them today, have been popular in America for the last hundred years or so. If you prefer the piecrust to remain on the crisp side, serve the pie fairly soon after the filling has firmed up.

PREP: 35 MINUTES PLUS COOLING AND CHILLING   BAKE: 10 MINUTES
MAKES 10 SERVINGS

Chocolate Wafer–Crumb Crust
 (page 105)
3/4 cup sugar
1/3 cup cornstarch
1/2 teaspoon salt
3 3/4 cups milk
5 large egg yolks

3 squares (3 ounces) unsweetened
 chocolate, melted
2 tablespoons butter or margarine,
 cut into pieces
2 teaspoons vanilla extract
Chocolate Curls (page 230; optional)
1 cup heavy or whipping cream

1. Prepare crust as directed. Cool.

2. Meanwhile, in heavy 3-quart saucepan, combine sugar, cornstarch, and salt; with wire whisk, stir in milk until smooth. Cook over medium heat, stirring constantly, until mixture has thickened and boils; boil 1 minute. In small bowl, with wire whisk, lightly beat egg yolks. Beat 1/2 cup hot milk mixture into beaten egg yolks. Slowly pour egg-yolk mixture back into milk mixture, stirring rapidly to prevent curdling. Cook over low heat, stirring constantly, until mixture is very thick or temperature on thermometer reaches 160°F.

3. Remove saucepan from heat; stir in melted chocolate, butter, and vanilla until butter has melted and mixture is smooth. Pour hot chocolate filling into cooled crust; press plastic wrap onto surface. Refrigerate until filling is set, about 4 hours.

4. Meanwhile, make Chocolate Curls, if using.

5. To serve, in small bowl, with mixer at medium speed, beat cream until stiff peaks form; spoon over chocolate filling. Top with chocolate curls, if desired.

Each serving: About 417 calories, 7g protein, 38g carbohydrate, 28g total fat (16g saturated), 171mg cholesterol, 329mg sodium.

Black Bottom Pie

Deserving of its classic status, this pie is both rich and light; it is layered with rum and chocolate custards and topped with cream.

PREP: 40 MINUTES PLUS COOLING AND CHILLING   BAKE: 10 MINUTES
MAKES 10 SERVINGS

Chocolate Wafer–Crumb Crust
  (page 105) or Coconut Pastry
  Crust (page 106)
1 teaspoon unflavored gelatin
2 tablespoons cold water
1¹/₂ cups milk
³/₄ cup sugar

4 large egg yolks
2 squares (2 ounces) unsweetened
  chocolate, melted
¹/₂ teaspoon vanilla extract
2 teaspoons dark rum or 1 teaspoon
  vanilla extract
2 cups heavy or whipping cream

1. Prepare crust as directed. Cool completely.

2. In cup, evenly sprinkle gelatin over cold water; let stand 2 minutes to soften gelatin slightly.

3. Meanwhile, in 2-quart saucepan, combine milk and ¹/₂ cup sugar; cook over medium heat, stirring, until bubbles form around edge.

4. In small bowl, with wire whisk, lightly beat egg yolks. Beat about ¹/₃ cup hot milk mixture into egg yolks. Slowly pour egg-yolk mixture back into milk mixture, whisking rapidly to prevent curdling. Cook over low heat, stirring constantly, until mixture has thickened slightly and coats back of spoon, about 10 minutes. (Temperature on thermometer should reach about 160°F; do not boil, or mixture will curdle.)

5. Transfer 1 cup milk mixture to small bowl. Stir in melted chocolate and vanilla until blended. Pour into cooled crust; refrigerate.

6. Over low heat, add softened gelatin to remaining milk mixture in saucepan; stir until gelatin has completely dissolved. Remove from heat. Stir in rum. Cool to room temperature, stirring occasionally.

7. In bowl, with mixer, beat cream with remaining ¹/₄ cup sugar until stiff peaks form. Whisk half of whipped cream into cooled gelatin mixture. Refrigerate remaining whipped cream. Spoon gelatin-cream mixture over chocolate layer. Cover; refrigerate until firm, about 3 hours. To serve, mound remaining whipped cream over filling.

Each serving: About 409 calories, 5g protein, 31g carbohydrate, 31g total fat (18g saturated), 168mg cholesterol, 171mg sodium.

Georgia Chocolate-Pecan Pie

This sinfully rich creation will be a favorite with any chocolate lover.

PREP: 45 MINUTES PLUS COOLING   BAKE: 65 MINUTES
MAKES 12 SERVINGS

Pastry Dough for 1-Crust Pie
  (page 104)
4 tablespoons butter or margarine
2 squares (2 ounces) unsweetened
  chocolate
1³/4 cups pecan halves (7 ounces)

³/4 cup packed dark brown sugar
³/4 cup dark corn syrup
1 teaspoon vanilla extract
3 large eggs

1. Prepare dough as directed through chilling.

2. On lightly floured surface, with floured rolling pin, roll dough into 12-inch round. Gently roll dough round onto rolling pin and ease into 9-inch pie plate, gently pressing dough against side of plate. Trim edge, leaving 1-inch overhang. Fold overhang under; make decorative edge. Refrigerate or freeze until firm, 10 to 15 minutes.

3. Preheat oven to 425°F. In heavy 1-quart saucepan, melt butter and chocolate over low heat, stirring frequently, until smooth. Cool slightly.

4. Line pie shell with foil; fill with pie weights or dry beans. Bake 15 minutes. Remove foil with weights; bake until golden, 5 to 10 minutes longer. If shell puffs up during baking, gently press it down with back of spoon. Cool on wire rack. Turn oven control to 350°F.

5. Coarsely chop 1 cup pecans. In large bowl, with wire whisk, mix cooled chocolate mixture, brown sugar, corn syrup, vanilla, and eggs until blended. Stir in chopped pecans and remaining pecan halves.

6. Pour pecan mixture into cooled pie shell. Bake until filling is set around edges but center jiggles slightly, 45 to 50 minutes. Cool on wire rack at least 1 hour for easier slicing.

Each serving: About 395 calories, 5g protein, 43g carbohydrate, 24g total fat (4g saturated), 53mg cholesterol, 225mg sodium.

Fudge Pecan Pie

Serve this dense brownie-like pie with a generous bowl of softly whipped, bourbon-spiked cream.

PREP: 30 MINUTES PLUS COOLING   BAKE: 1 HOUR 5 MINUTES
MAKES 10 SERVINGS

PASTRY
1 1/2 cups all-purpose flour
1/2 teaspoon salt
4 tablespoons cold butter or margarine
1/4 cup vegetable shortening
3 to 5 tablespoons ice water

FILLING
4 tablespoons butter or margarine
2 squares (2 ounces) unsweetened chocolate
1 bottle (16 ounces) light corn syrup
4 large eggs
1 teaspoon vanilla extract
1/4 cup all-purpose flour
1/4 cup sugar
1/4 teaspoon salt
1 1/2 cups pecan halves

1. Prepare Pastry: In large bowl, combine flour and salt. With pastry blender or two knives used scissor-fashion, cut in butter and shortening until mixture resembles coarse crumbs.

2. Sprinkle in ice water, 1 tablespoon at a time, mixing lightly with fork after each addition, until dough is just moist enough to hold together. Shape dough into disk; wrap in plastic wrap. Refrigerate 30 minutes or up to overnight. If chilled overnight, let stand 30 minutes at room temperature before rolling.

3. Meanwhile, prepare Filling: In 4-quart saucepan, melt butter and chocolate over low heat, stirring frequently, until smooth. With wire whisk, mix in corn syrup, eggs, and vanilla. Gradually whisk in flour, sugar, and salt until blended.

4. Preheat oven to 350°F. On lightly floured surface, with floured rolling pin, roll dough into 13-inch round. Gently roll dough round onto rolling pin and ease into 9 1/2-inch deep-dish pie plate, gently pressing dough against side of plate. Trim edge, leaving 1-inch overhang. Fold overhang under; form high decorative edge.

5. Chop 1 cup pecans; sprinkle over crust. Carefully, pour chocolate mixture over pecans. Arrange remaining 1/2 cup pecan halves on top. Bake until filling is set and knife inserted 1 inch from edge comes out almost clean, 65 to 75 minutes. Cool on wire rack.

Each serving: About 520 calories, 7g protein, 59g carbohydrate, 30g total fat (8g saturated), 95mg cholesterol, 328mg sodium.

DECORATIVE PIE EDGE

A classic border is the perfect way to add a professional finish to homemade pies.

TO MAKE A CRIMPED EDGE: With kitchen shears, trim the dough edge, leaving a 1-inch overhang. Fold the overhang under; form a stand-up edge. Push one index finger against the inside edge of the rim; with the index finger and thumb of the other hand, pinch dough to flute. Repeat all around.

TO MAKE A ROPE EDGE: With kitchen shears, trim the dough edge, leaving a 1-inch overhang. Fold the overhang under; form a stand-up edge. Press thumb into dough edge at an angle, then pinch dough between thumb and knuckle of index finger. Place thumb in groove left by index finger; pinch as before. Repeat all around.

Chocolate Truffle Tart

So unbelievably decadent, one thin slice is all you'll need.

PREP: 20 MINUTES PLUS CHILLING AND COOLING   BAKE: 40 MINUTES
MAKES 12 SERVINGS

TART PASTRY

1 cup all-purpose flour
1/4 teaspoon salt
6 tablespoons cold butter or
   margarine, cut into pieces
1 tablespoon vegetable shortening
2 to 3 tablespoons ice water

CHOCOLATE FILLING

6 squares (6 ounces) semisweet
   chocolate, coarsely chopped
1/2 cup butter or margarine (1 stick)
1/4 cup sugar
1 teaspoon vanilla extract
3 large eggs
1/2 cup heavy or whipping cream

softly whipped cream (optional)
White Chocolate Hearts (page 234;
   optional)

1. Prepare Tart Pastry: In large bowl, combine flour and salt. With pastry blender or two knives used scissor-fashion, cut in butter and shortening until mixture resembles coarse crumbs.

2. Sprinkle in ice water, 1 tablespoon at a time, mixing lightly with a fork after each addition, until dough is just moist enough to hold together. Shape dough into disk; wrap in plastic wrap. Refrigerate 30 minutes or up to overnight. (If chilled overnight, let stand 30 minutes at room temperature before rolling.)

3. Preheat oven to 425°F. On lightly floured surface, with floured rolling pin, roll dough into 11-inch round. Gently roll dough round onto rolling pin and ease dough into 9-inch tart pan with removable bottom. Fold overhang in and press dough against side of pan so it extends 1/8 inch above rim. Refrigerate or freeze until firm, 10 to 15 minutes.

4. Line tart shell with foil; fill with pie weights or dry beans. Bake 15 minutes. Remove foil with weights; bake until golden, 5 to 10 minutes longer. If shell puffs up during baking, gently press it down with back of spoon. Cool in pan on wire rack. Turn oven control to 350°F.

5. Meanwhile, prepare Chocolate Filling: In heavy 2-quart saucepan, melt chocolate and butter over very low heat, stirring frequently, until

smooth. Add sugar and vanilla, stirring until sugar has dissolved. In small bowl, with wire whisk, lightly beat eggs and cream. Whisk ⅓ cup warm chocolate mixture into egg mixture; stir egg mixture back into chocolate mixture in saucepan until blended.

7. Pour warm chocolate filling into cooled tart shell. Bake until custard is set but center still jiggles slightly, about 20 minutes.

8. Cool in pan on wire rack. When cool, carefully remove side of pan. Refrigerate until chilled, about 4 hours. Decorate with white chocolate hearts, or serve with whipped cream, if desired.

Each serving: About 306 calories, 4g protein, 22g carbohydrate, 24g total fat (14g saturated), 103mg cholesterol, 206mg sodium.

Chocolate Truffle Tart with Hazelnut Crust

This luscious dessert combines a fragrant hazelnut crust with a rich and silky chocolate ganache filling.

PREP: 45 MINUTES PLUS CHILLING AND COOLING   BAKE: 53 MINUTES
MAKES 12 SERVINGS

HAZELNUT CRUST
1/2 cup hazelnuts (filberts), toasted
2 tablespoons sugar
1 1/4 cups all-purpose flour
1/2 teaspoon salt
1/2 cup cold butter (1 stick), cut into
   pieces (do not use margarine)
4 tablespoons ice water

CHOCOLATE FILLING
7 squares (7 ounces) semisweet
   chocolate

1 square (1 ounce) unsweetened
   chocolate
4 tablespoons butter
   (do not use margarine)
1/3 cup sugar
1 teaspoon vanilla extract
pinch salt
2/3 cup plus 1/2 cup heavy or
   whipping cream
3 large eggs

1. Prepare Hazelnut Crust: Preheat oven to 425°F. Reserve 8 whole hazelnuts for garnish. In food processor with knife blade attached, blend remaining hazelnuts with sugar until finely ground. Add flour and salt to nut mixture; pulse until blended. Scatter butter over flour; pulse just until mixture resembles coarse crumbs. With processor running, add ice water, 1 tablespoon at a time, processing until dough almost forms a ball. Shape dough into disk; wrap in plastic wrap. Refrigerate until firm, about 30 minutes.

2. On lightly floured surface, with floured rolling pin, roll dough into 14-inch round. Gently roll dough round onto rolling pin and ease into 11-inch round tart pan with removable bottom. Fold overhang in and press against side of tart pan to form a rim 1/8 inch above edge of pan. Refrigerate or freeze until firm, 10 to 20 minutes.

3. Line tart shell with foil and fill with pie weights or dry beans. Bake 20 minutes; remove foil with weights and bake until golden, 8 to 10 minutes longer. Cool tart shell in pan on wire rack. Turn oven control to 350°F.

4. Meanwhile, prepare Chocolate Filling: In heavy 3-quart saucepan, melt semisweet and unsweetened chocolates and butter over low heat, stirring frequently, until smooth. Stir in sugar, vanilla, and salt until well blended; remove from heat. In small bowl, with fork or wire whisk, lightly beat 2/3 cup cream with eggs until mixed. Gradually whisk cream mixture into chocolate mixture until blended.

5. Pour chocolate mixture into cooled tart shell. Bake until custard is just set (center will appear jiggly), 15 to 17 minutes. Cool on wire rack. Serve at room temperature or refrigerate up to 1 day. If refrigerated, let tart stand at room temperature 1 hour to soften before serving.

6. In small bowl, with mixer at medium speed, beat remaining 1/2 cup cream until stiff peaks form. Spoon 8 dollops of whipped cream around edge of tart; top each dollop with a reserved hazelnut.

Each serving: About 415 calories, 6g protein, 29g carbohydrate, 32g total fat (17g saturated), 118mg cholesterol, 260mg sodium.

TOASTING NUTS

Toasting nuts brings out their flavor, and in the case of nuts such as hazelnuts, allows the skins to be removed.

To toast almonds, pecans, walnuts, or hazelnuts, preheat the oven to 350°F. Spread the shelled nuts in a single layer on a cookie sheet. Bake, stirring occasionally, until lightly browned and fragrant, about 10 minutes. Toast hazelnuts until the skins begin to peel away. Let the nuts cool completely before chopping.

To skin hazelnuts, wrap the still-warm toasted nuts in a clean kitchen towel and let stand for about 10 minutes. Using the towel, rub off as much of the skins as possible (all of the skin may not come off).

Brownie Shortbread Tart

Buttery shortbread meets the ultimate chocolate filling for a perfect match! Bake the tart ahead and freeze up to a month—thaw at room temperature before serving.

PREP: 40 MINUTES PLUS CHILLING AND COOLING   BAKE: 40 MINUTES
MAKES 12 SERVINGS

Shortbread Crust (page 107)
6 tablespoons margarine or butter
3 squares (3 ounces) unsweetened chocolate
1/2 cup granulated sugar
1/2 cup packed light brown sugar

2 large eggs
3/4 cup all-purpose flour
1/8 teaspoon salt
1 teaspoon vanilla extract
3/4 cup pecans, coarsely chopped

1. Prepare crust as directed.

2. Preheat oven to 350°F.

3. Prepare brownie filling: In 3-quart saucepan, melt butter and chocolate over low heat, stirring frequently, until smooth. Remove from heat; stir in granulated and brown sugars. Stir in eggs, one at a time, stirring well after each addition. Stir in flour, salt, vanilla, and pecans until well blended. Spoon into baked crust; spread evenly.

4. Bake until top is set, 16 to 18 minutes. Cool tart in pan on wire rack 1 hour to serve warm, or cool completely to serve later.

Each serving: About 370 calories, 4g protein, 38g carbohydrate, 24g total fat (12g saturated), 74mg cholesterol, 185mg sodium.

Chocolate-Walnut Pie

Imagine an ultra-rich, walnutty fudge brownie baked in a shortbread crust. Sound good? Here's the recipe. All you have to decide is whether to serve it warm or cool, and whether to add a big spoonful of whipped cream or a scoop of vanilla or coffee ice cream.

PREP: 30 MINUTES PLUS COOLING   BAKE: 50 MINUTES
MAKES 12 SERVINGS

Shortbread Crust (page 107)
1/2 cup butter or margarine (1 stick)
3 squares (3 ounces) unsweetened chocolate
1/2 cup packed light brown sugar
1/2 cup granulated sugar
2 large eggs
3/4 cup all-purpose flour
1/8 teaspoon salt
1 teaspoon vanilla extract
3/4 cup walnuts, coarsely chopped

1. Prepare crust as directed.
2. Preheat oven to 325°F. In 3-quart saucepan, melt butter and chocolate over low heat, stirring frequently, until smooth. Remove from heat and stir in brown and granulated sugars until blended. Add eggs, one at a time, stirring well after each addition. Stir in flour, salt, vanilla, and walnuts until well blended. Pour into cooled baked piecrust.
3. Bake until top is just set, about 30 minutes. Cool on wire rack 1 hour to serve warm, or cool completely to serve later.

Each serving: About 385 calories, 5g protein, 39g carbohydrate, 25g total fat (13g saturated), 77mg cholesterol, 195mg sodium.

Chocolate-Caramel Walnut Tart

If you don't have the time to refrigerate the pastry for thirty minutes, you can pop it into the freezer and it will be firm enough to roll in about half the time. Just keep an eye on it so it doesn't freeze.

PREP: 40 MINUTES PLUS CHILLING AND COOLING   BAKE: 22 MINUTES
MAKES 12 SERVINGS

TART PASTRY
1¹/₂ cups all-purpose flour
¹/₄ teaspoon salt
¹/₂ cup cold butter or margarine
  (1 stick), cut into pieces
2 tablespoons vegetable shortening
3 to 5 tablespoons ice water

CHOCOLATE-CARAMEL FILLING
1 cup sugar
¹/₄ cup water
³/₄ cup heavy or whipping cream
2 bars (4 ounces each) bittersweet
  chocolate, coarsely chopped
2 tablespoons butter or margarine
2 cups walnuts (8 ounces), lightly
  toasted (page 97) and chopped
2 teaspoons vanilla extract
whipped cream and walnut halves

1. Prepare Tart Pastry: In large bowl, combine flour and salt. With pastry blender or two knives used scissor-fashion, cut in butter and shortening until mixture resembles coarse crumbs.

2. Sprinkle in ice water, 1 tablespoon at a time, mixing lightly with fork after each addition, until dough is just moist enough to hold together. Shape dough into disk. Wrap disk in plastic wrap. Refrigerate 30 minutes or up to overnight. (If chilled overnight, let stand at room temperature 30 minutes before rolling.)

3. On lightly floured surface, with floured rolling pin, roll dough into 14-inch round. Gently roll dough round onto rolling pin and ease into 11-inch round tart pan with removable bottom. Run small knife or rolling pin over rim of pan to remove excess dough. Refrigerate or freeze until firm, 10 to 30 minutes.

4. Preheat oven to 425°F. Line tart shell with foil; fill with pie weights or dry beans. Bake 12 minutes. Remove foil and weights; bake until golden, 10 to 12 minutes longer. If crust puffs up during baking, gently press it to tart pan with back of spoon. Cool tart shell in pan on wire rack.

5. Meanwhile, prepare Chocolate-Caramel Filling: In heavy 3-quart saucepan, heat sugar and water over medium-high heat until melted and amber in color, about 10 minutes, swirling pan occasionally. Remove from heat. Stir in cream until smooth caramel forms; stir in chocolate and butter until melted. Stir in chopped walnuts and vanilla.

6. Pour warm chocolate filling into cooled tart shell. Refrigerate until set, at least 3 hours. Remove side of pan to serve. Garnish with whipped cream and top with walnut halves.

Each serving: About 505 calories, 6g protein, 42g carbohydrate, 38g total fat (16g saturated), 48mg cholesterol, 160mg sodium.

No-Bake Chocolate Fudge Tart

Reach for this recipe when you want a decadent chocolate treat and you don't want to heat up your kitchen by turning on the oven. All of the cooking is done in the microwave, and the packaged chocolate piecrust doesn't get baked.

PREP: 10 MINUTES PLUS CHILLING   COOK: 1 1/2 MINUTES
MAKES 8 SERVINGS

3/4 cup half-and-half or light cream
3 tablespoons sugar
6 squares (6 ounces) semisweet
   chocolate, chopped
2 square (2 ounces) unsweetened
   chocolate, chopped

1 teaspoon vanilla extract
1 (6-ounce) ready-to-use chocolate
   cookie crust
1/2 cup heavy or whipping cream
chocolate shavings

1. In microwave-safe bowl, combine half-and-half and 2 tablespoons sugar. Heat mixture in microwave oven on High 1 1/2 minutes, or until very hot. Add semisweet and unsweetened chocolates and vanilla; stir until chocolates have melted; pour into crust. Cover and refrigerate at least 1 hour or up to 3 days.

2. To serve, in small bowl, with mixer at medium speed, beat heavy cream until soft peaks form. With spatula, spread whipped cream over chocolate filling. Garnish with chocolate shavings.

Each serving: About 350 calories, 4g protein, 34g carbohydrate, 24g total fat (12g saturated), 29mg cholesterol, 115mg sodium.

Chocolate Tartlets

If you don't have tartlet pans, not to worry. Mini muffin pans work just as well. Decorate the finished tartlets as simply or as elaborately as you like with fresh berries or sliced fruit, depending on what looks good at the market.

PREP: 50 MINUTES PLUS CHILLING, COOLING, AND STANDING
BAKE: 9 MINUTES   MAKES 36 TARTLETS

Pastry Dough for 1-Crust Pie
  (page 104)
3 tablespoons apricot jam
2 squares (2 ounces) semisweet
  chocolate
3 tablespoons plus 1/4 cup heavy or
  whipping cream

1 tablespoon butter or margarine,
  cut into pieces
1 teaspoon vanilla extract
1 teaspoon confectioners' sugar
Assorted berries, very thinly sliced
  kumquats, or chocolate shavings

1. Prepare dough as directed through chilling.

2. Preheat oven to 425°F. On lightly floured surface, with floured rolling pin, roll dough slightly less than 1/16 inch thick. With 2 1/2-inch round cutter, cut out 36 pastry rounds (if necessary, reroll scraps). Ease into 3 dozen mini muffin-pan cups or 1 3/4-inch tartlet pans, pressing dough onto bottoms and against sides of pans.

3. Bake tartlets until golden, 9 to 12 minutes. Cool in pans on wire rack. Remove tartlet shells from pans; spoon 1/4 teaspoon jam into each shell. In top of double boiler set over simmering water, melt chocolate with 3 tablespoons cream, stirring until smooth. Remove from heat; stir in butter until smooth. Stir in vanilla. Spoon mixture evenly into tartlets, covering jam. Let stand until set.

4. In small bowl, with mixer at medium speed, beat remaining 1/4 cup cream and confectioners' sugar until stiff peaks form. Spoon small dollop of cream onto center of each tartlet. Garnish with berries, kumquats, or chocolate shavings.

Each tartlet: About 60 calories, 1g protein, 5g carbohydrate, 4g total fat (2g saturated), 8mg cholesterol, 30mg sodium.

Pastry Dough for 1-Crust Pie

Chilling a piecrust before baking helps it retain its shape.

PREP: 15 MINUTES PLUS CHILLING
MAKES ENOUGH DOUGH FOR ONE 9-INCH CRUST

1¼ cups all-purpose flour
¼ teaspoon salt
4 tablespoons cold butter or
  margarine, cut into pieces

2 tablespoons vegetable shortening
3 to 5 tablespoons ice water

1. In large bowl, combine flour and salt. With pastry blender or two knives used scissor-fashion, cut in butter and shortening until mixture resembles coarse crumbs.

2. Sprinkle in ice water, 1 tablespoon at a time, mixing lightly with fork after each addition, until dough is just moist enough to hold together.

3. Shape dough into disk; wrap in plastic wrap. Refrigerate 30 minutes or up to overnight. (If chilled overnight, let stand 30 minutes at room temperature before rolling.)

4. On lightly floured surface, with floured rolling pin, roll dough into 12-inch round. Gently roll dough round onto rolling pin and ease into pie plate, gently pressing dough against side of plate.

5. Make decorative edge. Refrigerate or freeze until firm, 10 to 15 minutes. Fill and bake as directed in recipe.

Each 1/10th pastry: About 123 calories, 2g protein, 13g carbohydrate, 7g total fat (4g saturated), 12mg cholesterol, 104mg sodium.

Graham Cracker–Crumb Crust

For the freshest flavor, make your own cookie crumbs. Personalize your crusts by using your favorite cookies to make the crumbs.

PREP: 10 MINUTES   BAKE: 10 MINUTES
MAKES ONE 9-INCH CRUST

1 1/4 cups graham-cracker crumbs   4 tablespoons butter or margarine,
  (11 rectangular graham crackers)   melted
                                          1 tablespoon sugar

1. Preheat oven to 375°F.
2. In 9-inch pie plate, with fork, mix crumbs, melted butter, and sugar until crumbs are evenly moistened. Press mixture firmly onto bottom and up side of pie plate, making small rim.
3. Bake 10 minutes; cool on wire rack. Fill as recipe directs.

Each 1/10th crust: About 105 calories, 1g protein, 12g carbohydrate, 6g total fat (3g saturated), 12mg cholesterol, 137mg sodium.

Chocolate Wafer–Crumb Crust

Prepare as directed but substitute **1 1/4 cups chocolate-wafer crumbs (about 24 cookies)** for graham-cracker crumbs.

Each 1/10th crust: About 108 calories, 1g protein, 12g carbohydrate, 7g total fat (3g saturated), 13mg cholesterol, 130mg sodium.

Vanilla Wafer–Crumb Crust

Prepare as directed but substitute **1 1/4 cups vanilla-wafer crumbs (about 35 cookies)** for graham-cracker crumbs.

Each 1/10th crust: About 92 calories, 1g protein, 9g carbohydrate, 6g total fat (3g saturated), 12mg cholesterol, 80mg sodium.

Coconut Pastry Crust

Toast the coconut in a shallow pan in a 350°F oven for about 10 minutes, stirring frequently.

PREP: 10 MINUTES   BAKE: 20 MINUTES   MAKES ONE 9-INCH CRUST

1 cup all-purpose flour
1/2 cup flaked sweetened coconut, toasted
6 tablespoons cold butter or margarine, cut into pieces

2 tablespoons sugar
1 tablespoon cold water

1. Preheat oven to 375°F. Grease 9-inch pie plate.

2. In food processor with knife blade attached, combine flour, coconut, butter, sugar, and cold water. Pulse until dough just holds together. Press dough evenly into bottom and up side of prepared pie plate, making a small rim.

3. Bake 20 minutes, or until golden. Cover edge loosely with foil to prevent overbrowning if necessary during last 10 minutes of baking. Cool on wire rack. Fill as recipe directs.

Each 1/10 pastry: About 135 calories, 1g protein, 14g carbohydrate, 9g total fat (5g saturated), 0.5g fiber, 19mg cholesterol, 80mg sodium.

Shortbread Crust

PREP: 10 MINUTES PLUS CHILLING   BAKE: 20 MINUTES
MAKES ENOUGH DOUGH FOR ONE 9-INCH TART

3/4 cup all-purpose flour

1/3 cup cornstarch

1/2 cup butter (1 stick), softened
   (do not use margarine)

1/3 cup confectioners' sugar

1 teaspoon vanilla extract

1. Preheat oven to 350°F. In medium bowl, combine flour and cornstarch. In large bowl, with mixer at medium speed, beat butter and sugar until light and fluffy. Beat in vanilla. Reduce speed to low and beat in flower mixture just until evenly moistened and crumbs form.

2. Place crumbs in 9-inch tart pan with removable bottom. Place sheet of plastic wrap over crumbs and press to smooth evenly over bottom and up side of pan. Discard plastic wrap. With fork, prick bottom and side of tart shell at 1-inch intervals to prevent puffing and shrinking during baking. Refrigerate or freeze until firm, 10 to 15 minutes.

3. Bake crust until lightly browned, about 20 minutes. Transfer crust in pan to wire rack to cool.

Each 1/8th crust: About 185 calories, 1g protein, 19g carbohydrate, 12g total fat (7g saturated), 31mg cholesterol, 120mg sodium.

COOKIES & CONFECTIONS

C hocolate cookies are just like compliments: they're sweet and you can never have too many. Here you'll find our most irresistible brownies, cookies, truffles, and fudge.

Know Your Cookies

Bar Cookies are the easiest: mix the dough, spread into a pan, and bake.
Drop Cookies use a dough that is dropped by the spoonful onto cookie sheets.
Molded Cookies are made by shaping dough (often into balls) by hand.
Pressed Cookies are made by squeezing dough through a cookie press or pastry bag to create a specific shape.
Refrigerator Cookies (icebox cookies) are sliced from a chilled dough.
Cut-Out Cookies are made from a dough that is rolled out and cut into shapes with cookie cutters.

Cookie Sheet Smarts

Good-quality cookie sheets are one of the secrets to perfect cookies. Use heavy-gauge aluminum sheets that have a dull finish. Cookie sheets with a nonstick finish brown cookies more quickly. For even baking, you may need to lower the oven temperature by 25°F. Cookie sheets should be at least 2 inches smaller than your oven.

Baking for Success

• In most of our recipes, butter or margarine can be used, but for the best flavor and texture, use butter.

• After the flour is added, mix the dough just until blended.

• Grease cookie sheets (we prefer vegetable shortening) only if directed.

• Use a measuring spoon (or small ice-cream scoop) to scoop up equal portions of dough for cookies that bake up at the same time.

• For evenly baked cookies, bake one sheet of cookies at a time in the center of the oven. To bake two sheets, place them in the upper and lower thirds of the oven. Halfway through the baking, rotate the sheets from front to back and between the racks.

• Bake for the minimum suggested time, then check often for doneness.

• Unless a recipe directs otherwise, cool cookies briefly before transferring them to racks to cool completely. Cool bar cookies completely before cutting them.

• Store soft cookies and crisp cookies in separate containers with tight-fitting covers.

• Bar cookies should be stored in the pan they were baked in, tightly covered with foil or plastic wrap.

GH's Classic Brownies

These brownies are a *Good Housekeeping* classic for good reason—they're perfect. To easily remove the brownies from the baking pan, line the pan with heavy-duty foil, allowing the foil to extend over the rim of the pan. Then you can lift the brownies from the pan by gripping the foil.

PREP: 15 MINUTES PLUS COOLING   BAKE: 25 MINUTES
MAKES 24 BROWNIES

1¹/₄ cups all-purpose flour
¹/₂ teaspoon salt
³/₄ cup butter or margarine
   (1¹/₂ sticks)
4 squares (4 ounces) unsweetened
   chocolate

4 squares (4 ounces) semisweet
   chocolate
2 cups sugar
1 tablespoon vanilla extract
5 large eggs, lightly beaten

1. Preheat oven to 350°F. Grease 13" by 9" baking pan. In small bowl, combine flour and salt.

2. In 3-quart saucepan, melt butter and unsweetened and semisweet chocolates over low heat, stirring frequently, until smooth. Remove from heat; stir in sugar and vanilla. Add eggs; stir until well mixed. Stir flour mixture into chocolate mixture just until blended. Spread batter evenly in prepared pan.

3. Bake brownie until toothpick inserted 2 inches from edge comes out almost clean, about 25 minutes. Cool completely in pan on wire rack.

4. When cool, cut brownie lengthwise into 4 strips, then cut each strip crosswise into 6 pieces.

Each brownie: About 205 calories, 3g protein, 25g carbohydrate, 11g total fat (7g saturated), 61mg cholesterol, 125mg sodium.

Praline-Iced Brownies

Prepare GH's Classic Brownies as directed; cool. In 2-quart saucepan, heat **5 tablespoons butter or margarine** and **1/3 cup packed brown sugar** over medium-low heat until sugar has melted and mixture boils, stirring occasionally, about 5 minutes. Remove from heat. Whisk in **3 tablespoons bourbon or 1 tablespoon vanilla plus 2 tablespoons water** and **2 cups confectioners' sugar** until smooth. With small metal spatula, spread icing over cooled brownies; sprinkle with **1/2 cup pecans,** toasted (page 97) and chopped, pressing them in lightly so they adhere. Cut lengthwise into 8 strips, then cut each strip crosswise into 8 pieces. Makes 64 brownies.

Each brownie: About 110 calories, 1g protein, 14g carbohydrate, 6g total fat (3g saturated), 25mg cholesterol, 55mg sodium.

LINING PAN WITH FOIL

Turn the baking pan bottom side up. Cover the pan tightly with foil, shiny side out. Remove foil cover.

Turn the baking pan right side up and carefully fit the molded foil into it, smoothing foil to fit into the edges.

Small-Batch Brownies

What's changed about brownies since the 1920s? Serving size. Cut these brownies into petite squares as the original recipe directs, rather than the larger, diet-busting bars we've become accustomed to.

PREP: 20 MINUTES PLUS COOLING   BAKE: 20 MINUTES
MAKES 36 BROWNIES

1/2 cup all-purpose flour
1/4 teaspoon baking powder
1/4 teaspoon salt
4 tablespoons butter or margarine
2 squares (2 ounces) unsweetened
  chocolate

1 cup sugar
2 large eggs
1 teaspoon vanilla extract
1/2 cup walnuts, chopped

1. Preheat oven to 350°F. Grease 9-inch square baking pan. Line pan with foil; grease foil. In small bowl, combine flour, baking powder, and salt.

2. In heavy 2-quart saucepan, melt butter and chocolate over low heat, stirring frequently, until smooth. Remove from heat. With wire whisk, stir in sugar, eggs, and vanilla.

3. With wooden spoon, stir flour mixture into chocolate mixture until just blended; stir in nuts. Spread batter evenly in prepared pan.

4. Bake until toothpick inserted in center comes out almost clean, about 20 minutes.

5. Cool brownie in pan on wire rack at least 1 hour. Transfer with foil to cutting board. When cool, cut brownie into 6 strips, then cut each strip crosswise into 6 pieces.

Each brownie: About 60 calories, 1g protein, 8g carbohydrate, 4g total fat (2g saturated), 16mg cholesterol, 36mg sodium.

Cocoa Brownies

We love these easy saucepan brownies—so easy to whip up on the spur of the moment with pantry staples.

PREP: 10 MINUTES PLUS COOLING   BAKE: 25 MINUTES
MAKES 16 BROWNIES

1/2 cup all-purpose flour	1 cup sugar
1/2 cup unsweetened cocoa	2 large eggs
1/4 teaspoon baking powder	1 teaspoon vanilla extract
1/4 teaspoon salt	1 cup walnuts (4 ounces),
1/2 cup butter or margarine (1 stick)	coarsely chopped (optional)

1. Preheat oven to 350°F. Grease 9-inch square baking pan. In small bowl, combine flour, cocoa, baking powder, and salt.

2. In 3-quart saucepan, melt butter over low heat. Remove from heat and stir in sugar. Stir in eggs, one at a time, until well blended; add vanilla. Stir flour mixture into sugar mixture until blended. Stir in nuts, if using. Spread batter evenly in prepared pan.

3. Bake until toothpick inserted 2 inches from center comes out almost clean, about 25 minutes. Cool completely in pan on wire rack.

4. When cool, cut brownie into 4 strips, then cut each strip crosswise into 4 pieces.

Each brownie: About 132 calories, 2g protein, 17g carbohydrate, 7g total fat (4g saturated), 42mg cholesterol, 110mg sodium.

Fudgy Lowfat Brownies

Moist, chocolaty, and lowfat. Need we say more? Serve with cold skim milk for a healthful and delicious treat.

PREP: 15 MINUTES PLUS COOLING BAKE: 18 MINUTES
MAKES 16 BROWNIES

1 teaspoon instant espresso-coffee powder
1 teaspoon hot water
3/4 cup all-purpose flour
1/2 cup unsweetened cocoa
1/2 teaspoon baking powder

1/4 teaspoon salt
3 tablespoons butter or margarine
3/4 cup sugar
2 large egg whites
1/4 cup dark corn syrup
1 teaspoon vanilla extract

1. Preheat oven to 350°F. Grease 8-inch square baking pan. In cup, dissolve espresso powder in hot water. In medium bowl, combine flour, cocoa, baking powder, and salt.

2. In 2-quart saucepan, melt butter over low heat. Remove from heat. With wooden spoon, stir in sugar, egg whites, corn syrup, espresso, and vanilla until blended. Stir sugar mixture into flour mixture just until blended (do not overmix). Pour batter evenly into prepared pan.

3. Bake until toothpick inserted in center comes out almost clean, 18 to 22 minutes. Cool brownie completely in pan on wire rack.

4. When cool, cut brownie into 4 strips, then cut each strip crosswise into 4 pieces. If brownie is difficult to cut, use knife dipped in hot water and dried; repeat as necessary.

Each brownie: About 103 calories, 2g protein, 19g carbohydrate, 3g total fat (2g saturated), 6mg cholesterol, 88mg sodium.

Cocoa Brownies
with Brown Butter Frosting

Did you know that baked goods made with cocoa often have a richer chocolate flavor than those made with chocolate? Here a generous amount of cocoa—three-quarters of a cup—makes these extra chocolaty.

PREP: 25 MINUTES PLUS COOLING   BAKE: 18 MINUTES
MAKES 24 BROWNIES

BROWNIE
1 cup all-purpose flour
3/4 cup unsweetened cocoa
1/2 teaspoon baking powder
1/2 teaspoon salt
3/4 cup butter or margarine
  (11/2 sticks)
11/2 cups granulated sugar
2 teaspoons vanilla extract
4 large eggs

BROWN BUTTER FROSTING
4 tablespoons butter
  (do not use margarine)
2 cups confectioners' sugar
3 tablespoons milk
1 teaspoon vanilla extract

1. Preheat oven to 350°F. Grease 13" by 9" baking pan.

2. Prepare Brownie: In medium bowl, combine flour, cocoa, baking powder, and salt. In 3-quart saucepan, melt butter over low heat. Remove from heat; stir in granulated sugar and vanilla. Add eggs, one at a time, stirring until well blended. Stir flour mixture into sugar mixture just until blended. Spread batter evenly in prepared pan.

3. Bake brownie until toothpick inserted 2 inches from edge comes out almost clean, 18 to 22 minutes. Cool in pan on wire rack.

4. When brownie is cool, prepare Brown Butter Frosting: In 2-quart saucepan, cook butter over medium heat, stirring occasionally, until lightly browned, 5 to 6 minutes. Remove from heat. With wooden spoon, stir in confectioners' sugar, milk, and vanilla until smooth.

5. With small metal spatula, spread frosting over cooled brownies. Cut lengthwise into 4 strips, then cut each strip crosswise into 6 pieces.

Each brownie: About 195 calories, 2g protein, 28g carbohydrate, 9g total fat (6g saturated), 58mg cholesterol, 150mg sodium.

Milk Chocolate-Glazed Brownies

Be sure to let the brownies cool completely before preparing the milk chocolate glaze.

Prep: 20 minutes plus cooling   Bake: 30 minutes
Makes 24 brownies

BROWNIE
1¼ cups all-purpose flour
½ teaspoon salt
¾ cup butter or margarine
  (1½ sticks)
1 bar (7 ounces) milk chocolate
3 squares (3 ounces) semisweet
  chocolate

1½ cups sugar
5 large eggs
2 teaspoons vanilla extract

MILK CHOCOLATE GLAZE
1 cup milk chocolate chips
  (6 ounces)
4 tablespoons butter or margarine
1 teaspoon vanilla extract

1. Preheat oven to 350°F. Grease 13" by 9" baking pan.

2. Prepare Brownie: In small bowl, combine flour and salt. In 3-quart saucepan, melt butter and chocolate over low heat, stirring frequently, until smooth.

3. Meanwhile, in medium bowl, with wire whisk, stir sugar, eggs, and vanilla until combined. Stir in flour mixture. Stir egg mixture into chocolate mixture until well blended. Spread batter evenly in prepared pan.

4. Bake until toothpick inserted 2 inches from edge comes out almost clean, 30 to 35 minutes. Cool in pan on wire rack.

5. When brownie is cool, prepare Milk Chocolate Glaze: In 1-quart saucepan, melt chocolate and butter over low heat, stirring frequently, until smooth. Remove from heat; stir in vanilla.

6. With small metal spatula, spread glaze over cooled brownie. Cut lengthwise into 4 strips, then cut each strip crosswise into 6 pieces.

Each brownie: About 260 calories, 3g protein, 28g carbohydrate, 15g total fat (6g saturated), 70mg cholesterol, 160mg sodium.

Mexican Brownies

These luscious brownies made with cocoa have a hint of cinnamon and are topped with a creamy coffee-accented frosting.

PREP: 30 MINUTES PLUS COOLING   BAKE: 25 MINUTES
MAKES 24 BROWNIES

BROWNIE
1 cup all-purpose flour
1 cup unsweetened cocoa
1/2 teaspoon baking powder
1/2 teaspoon ground cinnamon
1/2 teaspoon salt
1 cup butter or margarine (2 sticks)
2 cups granulated sugar
4 large eggs
1 tablespoon vanilla extract

COFFEE FROSTING
1 tablespoon instant coffee powder
   or granules
2 tablespoons water
1 tablespoon vanilla extract
1/4 cup packed brown sugar
3 tablespoons butter or margarine
1 1/3 cups confectioners' sugar
coffee beans and/or chopped
   semisweet chocolate

1. Preheat oven to 350°F. Grease 13" by 9" baking pan. Line pan with foil; grease foil.

2. In medium bowl, combine flour, cocoa, baking powder, cinnamon, and salt.

3. In 3-quart saucepan, melt butter over low heat. Remove from heat; stir in granulated sugar. Stir in eggs, one at a time, until well blended; add vanilla. Stir flour mixture into sugar mixture until blended. Spread batter evenly in prepared pan.

4. Bake until toothpick inserted in center of pan comes out almost clean, 25 to 30 minutes. Cool completely in pan on wire rack.

5. When brownie is cool, prepare Coffee Frosting: In cup, dissolve coffee in water and vanilla; set aside. In 1-quart saucepan, heat brown sugar and butter over medium heat until mixture melts and bubbles, about 2 minutes. Remove pan from heat. With wire whisk, stir in coffee mixture; stir in confectioners' sugar until blended and smooth.

6. With small metal spatula, spread warm frosting over cooled brownie. Let stand 20 minutes to allow frosting to set slightly. Cut lengthwise into 4 strips, then cut each strip crosswise into 6 pieces. Garnish each brownie with a coffee bean or chopped chocolate.

Each brownie: About 225 calories, 2g protein, 31g carbohydrate, 11g total fat (7g saturated), 61mg cholesterol, 165mg sodium.

Mint-Chocolate Brownies

A double dose of mint makes these brownies a winner: the brownie batter is laden with halved mint-chocolate candies and the icing has a touch of crème de menthe liqueur.

PREP: 25 MINUTES PLUS COOLING   BAKE: 25 MINUTES
MAKES 24 BROWNIES

BROWNIE
1¼ cups all-purpose flour
½ teaspoon salt
¾ cup butter or margarine
  (1½ sticks)
4 squares (4 ounces) semisweet
  chocolate
4 squares (4 ounces) unsweetened
  chocolate
2 cups sugar
1 tablespoon vanilla extract

5 large eggs, lightly beaten
1 package (4.67 ounces) chocolate
  and mint–layered candies (about
  1 cup), each broken in half

MINT-CHOCOLATE ICING
1 package (6 ounces) semisweet
  chocolate chips (1 cup)
4 tablespoons butter or margarine
1 tablespoon crème de menthe

1. Preheat oven to 350°F. Grease 13" by 9" baking pan.

2. Prepare Brownie: In small bowl, combine flour and salt. In 3-quart saucepan, melt butter and semisweet and unsweetened chocolates over low heat, stirring frequently, until smooth. Remove from heat; stir in sugar and vanilla. Add eggs; stir until well mixed. Stir in mint candies. Stir flour mixture into chocolate mixture just until blended. Spread batter evenly in prepared pan.

3. Bake brownie until toothpick inserted 2 inches from edge comes out almost clean, 25 to 30 minutes. Cool in pan on wire rack.

4. When brownie is cool, prepare Mint-Chocolate Icing: In small microwave-safe bowl, heat chocolate and butter on High 30 seconds; stir in crème de menthe until well blended.

5. With small spatula, spread icing over cooled brownie. Set aside to allow icing to set.

6. Cut brownie lengthwise into 4 strips, then cut each strip crosswise into 6 pieces.

Each brownie: About 280 calories, 4g protein, 34g carbohydrate, 16g total fat (10g saturated), 66mg cholesterol, 145mg sodium.

Mochaccino Brownies

Mocha is the combination of coffee and chocolate, while a mochaccino is a cappuccino with chocolate syrup added.

PREP: 25 MINUTES PLUS COOLING   BAKE: 25 MINUTES
MAKES 24 BROWNIES

BROWNIE
1 cup all-purpose flour
1/4 teaspoon salt
2 tablespoons instant- or espresso-
  coffee powder
1 tablespoon very hot water
1/2 cup butter or margarine (1 stick)
1 package (8 ounces) unsweetened
  chocolate squares
2 cups granulated sugar
4 large eggs, lightly beaten
1 teaspoon vanilla extract

MOCHACCINO GLAZE
4 teaspoons instant- or espresso-
  coffee powder
2 tablespoons butter or margarine,
  melted and kept hot
2 cups confectioners' sugar
3 tablespoons milk
1 teaspoon vanilla extract

1. Preheat oven to 350°F. Grease 13"by 9" baking pan.

2. Prepare Brownie: In small bowl, combine flour and salt. In cup, dissolve coffee in water; set aside. In 3-quart saucepan, melt butter and chocolate over low heat, stirring frequently, until smooth. Remove from heat; stir in granulated sugar. Add eggs, vanilla, and coffee mixture; stir until blended. Stir flour mixture into chocolate mixture just until blended. Spread batter evenly in prepared pan.

3. Bake brownie until toothpick inserted 2 inches from edge comes out almost clean, 25 to 30 minutes. Cool in pan on wire rack.

4. When brownie is cool; prepare Mochaccino Glaze: In medium bowl, with wire whisk, stir coffee and hot melted butter until coffee has dissolved. Stir in confectioners' sugar, milk, and vanilla until smooth.

5. With small metal spatula, spread glaze over cooled brownie. Cut lengthwise into 4 strips, then cut each strip crosswise into 6 pieces.

Each brownie: About 230 calories, 3g protein, 33g carbohydrate, 11g total fat (9g saturated), 49mg cholesterol, 90mg sodium.

Malted Milk Bars

Milkshake fans will adore these superlative bars. The frosting is made with malted milk powder and sprinkled with chopped malted milk balls.

PREP: 15 MINUTES PLUS COOLING   BAKE: 25 MINUTES
MAKES 32 BARS

CHOCOLATE BASE
1 1/2 cups all-purpose flour
1/2 teaspoon baking powder
1/2 teaspoon salt
3/4 cup butter or margarine
   (1 1/2 sticks)
4 squares (4 ounces) semisweet
   chocolate
2 squares (2 ounces) unsweetened
   chocolate
1 1/2 cups granulated sugar
1 tablespoon vanilla extract
4 large eggs, lightly beaten

MALTED MILK TOPPING
3/4 cup malted milk powder
3 tablespoons milk
1 teaspoon vanilla extract
3 tablespoons butter or margarine,
   softened
1 cup confectioners' sugar
1 1/2 cups malted milk ball candies
   (about 5 ounces), coarsely chopped

1. Preheat oven to 350°F. Grease 13" by 9" baking pan. Line pan with foil, extending foil over rim; grease foil. In small bowl, combine flour, baking powder, and salt.

2. Prepare Chocolate Base: In heavy 3-quart saucepan, melt butter and semisweet and unsweetened chocolates over low heat, stirring frequently, until smooth. Remove from heat. With wooden spoon, stir in granulated sugar and vanilla. Beat in eggs until well blended. Stir flour mixture into chocolate mixture until blended. Spread batter evenly in prepared pan.

3. Bake until toothpick inserted 1 inch from edge of pan comes out clean, 25 to 30 minutes. Cool in pan on wire rack.

4. Prepare Malted Milk Topping: In small bowl, stir malted milk powder, milk, and vanilla until blended. Stir in butter and confectioners' sugar until blended. With small metal spatula, spread topping over cooled chocolate base; top with chopped malted milk ball candies; allow topping to set.

5. When topping is set, transfer base with foil to cutting board. Cut lengthwise into 4 strips, then cut each strip crosswise into 8 pieces.

Each bar: About 200 calories, 3g protein, 27g carbohydrate, 10g total fat (5g saturated), 42mg cholesterol, 155mg sodium.

Hazelnut Brownies

Nutella is a chocolate-hazelnut spread that was created in Italy in the 1940s by Pietro Ferrero. At that time, chocolate was in short supply due to the war, so he stretched what he had by adding ground hazelnuts, creating a spread that became hugely popular. It is now found in supermarkets, usually near the peanut butter. Try it on toast for a breakfast treat.

PREP: 30 MINUTES PLUS COOLING   BAKE: 25 MINUTES
MAKES 24 BROWNIES

1 cup all-purpose flour
1/2 teaspoon salt
3/4 cup butter or margarine
  (11/2 sticks)
4 squares (4 ounces) unsweetened
  chocolate
2 squares (2 ounces) semisweet
  chocolate

1/2 cup chocolate-hazelnut spread
  (about half 13-ounce jar)
11/2 cups sugar
1 teaspoon vanilla extract
4 large eggs, lightly beaten
1 cup hazelnuts (filberts; 4 ounces),
  toasted (page 97) and coarsely
  chopped

1. Preheat oven to 350°F. Grease 13" by 9" baking pan. In small bowl, combine flour and salt.

2. In 3-quart saucepan, melt butter and unsweetened and semisweet chocolates over low heat, stirring frequently, until smooth.

3. Remove saucepan from heat; stir in hazelnut spread. Add sugar and vanilla; stir until well blended. Add eggs; stir until well mixed. Stir in flour mixture and hazelnuts, just until blended. Spread batter evenly in prepared pan.

4. Bake until toothpick inserted 2 inches from edge comes out almost clean, 25 to 30 minutes. Cool in pan on wire rack.

5. When cool, cut brownie lengthwise into 4 strips, then cut each strip crosswise into 6 pieces.

Each brownie: About 230 calories, 4g protein, 23g carbohydrate, 15g total fat (6g saturated), 52mg cholesterol, 125mg sodium.

Caramel-Nut Brownies

Ultrarich brownies that have all the flavor of the popular candy known as turtles: nuts, caramel, and chocolate.

PREP: 20 MINUTES PLUS COOLING   BAKE: 25 MINUTES
MAKES 24 SERVINGS

1 cup all-purpose flour	1 cup packed light brown sugar
1/2 teaspoon salt	3 large eggs, lightly beaten
3/4 cup butter or margarine	1 teaspoon vanilla extract
(11/2 sticks)	1/2 cup walnuts, coarsely chopped
4 squares (4 ounces) unsweetened	1 cup individually wrapped caramels
chocolate	(about 25), unwrapped and each
1 cup granulated sugar	cut in half

1. Preheat oven to 350°F. Grease 13" by 9" baking pan. In small bowl, combine flour and salt.

2. In 3-quart saucepan, melt butter and chocolate over low heat, stirring frequently, until smooth. Remove from heat; stir in granulated and brown sugars and eggs until well mixed. Stir in vanilla. Stir flour mixture into chocolate mixture just until blended; stir in walnuts. Spread batter evenly in prepared pan; sprinkle with caramels.

3. Bake brownie until toothpick inserted 2 inches from edge comes out almost clean, 25 to 30 minutes. Cool in pan on wire rack.

4. When cool, cut brownie lengthwise into 4 strips, then cut each strip crosswise into 6 pieces.

Each brownie: About 220 calories, 3g protein, 28g carbohydrate, 12g total fat (6g saturated), 43mg cholesterol, 140mg sodium.

This recipe was tested with several different brands of caramels and, to our surprise, had varying results. For soft, gooey caramels in the baked brownie (our test kitchen's preference) buy a brand that lists sweetened condensed milk as its first ingredient. If you prefer the caramels to be firm and chewy, buy a brand that lists corn syrup or glucose syrup first.

Rocky Road Brownies

The original rocky road treat was a chocolate candy over which miniature marshmallows and nuts were scattered, and its name is derived from its resemblance to a bumpy road. Since then, rocky road cakes, pies, tarts, and even brownies have been created and embraced.

PREP: 30 MINUTES PLUS COOLING   BAKE: 25 MINUTES
MAKES 24 BROWNIES

1¼ cups all-purpose flour
½ teaspoon baking powder
½ teaspoon salt
¾ cup butter or margarine
  (1½ sticks)
6 squares (6 ounces) unsweetened
  chocolate

2 cups sugar
2 teaspoons vanilla extract
5 large eggs, lightly beaten
2 cups miniature marshmallows
1½ cups assorted nuts (6 ounces),
  toasted (page 97) and coarsely
  chopped

1. Preheat oven to 350°F. Grease 13" by 9" baking pan. Line pan with foil; grease foil. In small bowl, combine flour, baking powder, and salt.

2. In 3-quart saucepan, melt butter and chocolate over low heat, stirring frequently until smooth. Remove from heat; stir in sugar and vanilla. Add eggs; stir until well blended. Stir flour mixture into chocolate mixture just until blended. Spread batter evenly in prepared pan.

3. Bake until toothpick inserted 2 inches from edge comes out almost clean, about 20 minutes. Sprinkle top of brownie evenly with marshmallows; top with nuts. Bake until marshmallows melt slightly, about 5 minutes longer. Cool in pan on wire rack.

4. When cool, cut brownie lengthwise into 4 strips, then cut each strip crosswise into 6 pieces.

Each brownie: About 255 calories, 5g protein, 29g carbohydrate, 15g total fat (7g saturated), 61mg cholesterol, 150mg sodium.

Peanut Butter Swirl Brownies

For the prettiest swirls, twist the knife just enough to create a bold pattern.

PREP: 30 MINUTES PLUS COOLING   BAKE: 30 MINUTES
MAKES 24 BROWNIES

BROWNIE

1 1/4 cups all-purpose flour
3/4 teaspoon baking powder
1/2 teaspoon salt
1/2 cup butter or margarine (1 stick)
4 squares (4 ounces) unsweetened chocolate
4 squares (4 ounces) semisweet chocolate
1 1/2 cups sugar
4 large eggs, lightly beaten
2 teaspoons vanilla extract

PEANUT BUTTER SWIRL

1 cup creamy peanut butter
4 tablespoons butter or margarine, softened
1/3 cup sugar
2 tablespoons all-purpose flour
1 large egg
1 teaspoon vanilla extract

1. Preheat oven to 350°F. Grease 13" by 9" baking pan.

2. Prepare Brownie: In small bowl, combine flour, baking powder, and salt. In 3-quart saucepan, melt butter and unsweetened and semisweet chocolates over low heat, stirring frequently, until smooth. Remove from heat; stir in sugar. Add eggs and vanilla; stir until well mixed. Stir flour mixture into chocolate mixture until blended.

3. Prepare Peanut Butter Swirl: In medium bowl, with mixer at medium speed, beat peanut butter, butter, sugar, flour, egg, and vanilla until well blended.

4. Spread 2 cups chocolate batter in pan; top with 6 large dollops of peanut butter mixture. Spoon remaining chocolate batter over and between peanut butter in 6 large dollops. With tip of knife, cut and twist through mixtures to create swirled effect.

5. Bake until toothpick inserted 2 inches from edge comes out almost clean, 30 to 35 minutes. Cool in pan on wire rack.

6. When cool, cut brownie lengthwise into 4 strips, then cut each strip crosswise into 6 pieces.

Each brownie: About 265 calories, 6g protein, 26g carbohydrate, 17g total fat (8g saturated), 61mg cholesterol, 185mg sodium.

Black Forest Brownies

Kirsch, sour cherries, and chocolate are the hallmarks of Black Forest cake, which was originally created in the Black Forest region of Germany. We've captured all the fabulous flavor of the classic in a brownie that takes less than twenty minutes to prepare.

PREP: 20 MINUTES PLUS COOLING   BAKE: 25 MINUTES
MAKES 24 BROWNIES

1 cup all-purpose flour
1/2 teaspoon salt
3/4 cup butter or margarine
   (11/2 sticks)
1/2 cup unsweetened cocoa
2 tablespoons kirsch (cherry-flavored
   liqueur), optional

13/4 cups sugar
3 teaspoons vanilla extract
4 large eggs, lightly beaten
3/4 cup dried tart cherries
1 container (16 ounces) sour cream

1. Preheat oven to 350°F. Grease 13" by 9" baking pan. In small bowl, combine flour and salt.

2. In 3-quart saucepan, melt butter over low heat. Remove from heat; with wire whisk, stir in cocoa until smooth. Add kirsch, if using, 1 1/2 cups sugar, and 2 teaspoons vanilla, whisking until well mixed. Add eggs; stir until well combined. Stir flour mixture into cocoa mixture just until blended; stir in cherries. Spread batter evenly in prepared pan.

3. Bake until toothpick inserted 1 inch from edge comes out almost clean, 20 to 25 minutes.

4. Meanwhile, in small bowl, stir sour cream, remaining 1/4 cup sugar, and remaining 1 teaspoon vanilla until blended. With small metal spatula, spread sour cream mixture evenly over baked brownie. Bake until topping has set, about 5 minutes longer. Cool completely in pan on wire rack.

5. When cool, cut brownie lengthwise into 4 strips, then cut each strip crosswise into 6 pieces.

Each brownie: About 200 calories, 3g protein, 23g carbohydrate, 11g total fat (7g saturated), 60mg cholesterol, 130mg sodium.

Raspberry Brownies

Raspberries and chocolate are a lovely combination. We suggest using seedless raspberry jam, but if you have raspberry jam with seeds in your pantry, press it through a coarse sieve to remove the seeds.

PREP: 20 MINUTES PLUS COOLING   BAKE: 30 MINUTES
MAKES 36 BROWNIES

1 cup all-purpose flour	1½ cups sugar
¾ cup unsweetened cocoa	4 large eggs
½ teaspoon baking powder	¾ cup seedless raspberry jam
½ teaspoon salt	2 teaspoons vanilla extract
1 cup butter or margarine (2 sticks)	

1. Preheat oven to 350°F. Grease 13" by 9" baking pan. In small bowl, combine flour, cocoa, baking powder, and salt.

2. In 3-quart saucepan, melt butter over low heat. Remove from heat; with wire whisk, stir in sugar. Add eggs, one at a time, beating well after each addition. Stir in jam and vanilla, whisking until well mixed. With spoon, stir flour mixture into butter mixture just until blended. Spread batter evenly in prepared pan.

3. Bake brownie until toothpick inserted 2 inches from edge comes out almost clean, 30 to 35 minutes. Cool in pan on wire rack.

4. When cool, cut brownie lengthwise into 6 strips, then cut each strip crosswise into 6 pieces.

Each brownie: About 125 calories, 2g protein, 16g carbohydrate, 6g total fat (4g saturated), 38mg cholesterol, 105mg sodium.

Gooey St. Louis Brownies

These brownies have two layers: a deep chocolate base and a sweet cream-cheese topping that is spread over the brownie base before they are baked. For easy cutting, lightly spray the knife with cooking spray or dip it into hot water, shaking off the excess.

PREP: 25 MINUTES PLUS COOLING   BAKE: 55 MINUTES
MAKES 36 BROWNIES

BROWNIE
1 1/4 cups all-purpose flour
1/2 teaspoon salt
3/4 cup butter or margarine
  (1 1/2 sticks)
6 squares (6 ounces) unsweetened
  chocolate
2 cups granulated sugar
1 teaspoon vanilla extract
3 large eggs, lightly beaten

GOOEY TOPPING
1 package (8 ounces) cream cheese,
  softened
2 large eggs
2 cups confectioners' sugar
1 teaspoon vanilla extract

1. Preheat oven to 350°F. Grease 13"by 9" baking pan.
2. Prepare Brownie: In small bowl, combine flour and salt. In 3-quart saucepan, melt butter and chocolate over low heat, stirring frequently, until smooth. Remove from heat; stir in granulated sugar and vanilla. Add eggs; stir until well blended. Stir flour mixture into chocolate mixture just until blended. Spread batter evenly in prepared pan.
3. Prepare Gooey Topping: In medium bowl, with mixer at low speed, beat cream cheese, eggs, confectioners' sugar, and vanilla until well combined. With small metal spatula, gently spread topping over brownie.
4. Bake until toothpick inserted 2 inches from edge comes out almost clean and top turns golden brown, 55 to 60 minutes. Cool in pan on wire rack.
5. When cool, cut brownie lengthwise into 6 strips, then cut each strip crosswise into 6 pieces.

Each brownie: About 175 calories, 3g protein, 22g carbohydrate, 9g total fat (6g saturated), 47mg cholesterol, 100mg sodium.

Almond Cheesecake Brownies

These sinfully rich brownies are marbled with a ribbon of cheesecake.

PREP: 30 MINUTES PLUS COOLING   BAKE: 35 MINUTES
MAKES 24 BROWNIES

1¼ cups all-purpose flour
¾ teaspoon baking powder
½ teaspoon salt
½ cup butter or margarine (1 stick)
4 squares (4 ounces) semisweet
   chocolate, chopped
4 squares (4 ounces) unsweetened
   chocolate, chopped

2 cups sugar
5 large eggs
2½ teaspoons vanilla extract
1½ packages (8 ounces each)
   cold cream cheese
¾ teaspoon almond extract

1. Preheat oven to 350°F. Grease 13" by 9" baking pan. In small bowl, combine flour, baking powder, and salt.

2. In heavy 4-quart saucepan, melt butter and semisweet and unsweetened chocolates over low heat, stirring frequently, until smooth. Remove from heat. With wooden spoon, beat in 1½ cups sugar. Add 4 eggs and 2 teaspoons vanilla; beat until well blended. Stir flour mixture into chocolate mixture just until blended.

3. In small bowl, with mixer at medium speed, beat cream cheese until smooth; gradually beat in remaining ½ cup sugar. Beat in remaining egg, almond extract, and remaining ½ teaspoon vanilla just until blended.

4. Spread 1½ cups chocolate batter in prepared pan. Spoon cream-cheese mixture in 6 large dollops on top of chocolate mixture (cream-cheese mixture will cover most of chocolate batter). Spoon remaining chocolate batter over and between cream cheese in 6 large dollops. With tip of knife, cut and twist through mixtures to create marbled effect.

5. Bake until toothpick inserted in center comes out almost clean, 35 to 40 minutes. Cool completely in pan on wire rack.

6. When cool, cut brownie lengthwise into 4 strips, then cut each strip crosswise into 6 pieces.

Each brownie: About 238 calories, 4g protein, 26g carbohydrate, 14g total fat (8g saturated), 70mg cholesterol, 159mg sodium.

Almond Lattice Brownies

A rich almond paste topping is piped over brownie batter before it is baked.

PREP: 25 MINUTES PLUS COOLING   BAKE: 25 MINUTES
MAKES 24 BROWNIES

BROWNIE
1¼ cups all-purpose flour
½ teaspoon salt
½ cup butter or margarine (1 stick)
4 squares (4 ounces) semisweet
  chocolate
4 squares (4 ounces) unsweetened
  chocolate
1½ cups sugar
2 teaspoons vanilla extract
3 large eggs, lightly beaten

ALMOND LATTICE TOPPING
1 tube or can (7 to 8 ounces) almond
  paste, crumbled
1 large egg
¼ cup sugar
1 tablespoon all-purpose flour
1 teaspoon vanilla extract

1. Preheat oven to 350°F. Grease 13" by 9" baking pan.

2. Prepare Brownie: In small bowl, combine flour and salt. In 3-quart saucepan, melt butter and semisweet and unsweetened chocolates over low heat, stirring frequently, until smooth. Remove from heat; stir in sugar and vanilla. Add eggs; stir until well mixed. Stir flour mixture into chocolate mixture just until blended. Spread batter evenly in prepared pan.

3. Prepare Almond Lattice Topping: In food processor with knife blade attached, pulse almond paste, egg, sugar, flour, and vanilla until mixture is smooth, scraping bowl with rubber spatula. Transfer almond mixture to small ziptight plastic bag. With scissors, cut bottom corner of bag on diagonal, ¼ inch from edge. Pipe almond topping over brownie batter to make 10 diagonal lines, spacing them 1 inch apart. Pipe remaining topping diagonally across first set of lines, to make 10 more lines and create a lattice design.

4. Bake until toothpick inserted 2 inches from edge comes out almost clean, 25 to 30 minutes. Cool in pan on wire rack.

5. When cool, cut brownie lengthwise into 4 strips, then cut each strip crosswise into 6 pieces.

Each brownie: About 220 calories, 4g protein, 28g carbohydrate, 11g total fat (5g saturated), 46mg cholesterol, 100mg sodium.

Chocolate Pecan Bars

If you have the extra time, toast the pecans in the oven for 5 to 10 minutes to bring out their rich flavor; cool before using.

PREP: 25 MINUTES   BAKE: 45 MINUTES   MAKES 32 BARS

CRUST
3/4 cup butter or margarine
  (11/2 sticks), softened
1/2 cup confectioners' sugar
2 cups all-purpose flour

FILLING
2 squares (2 ounces) semisweet
  chocolate

2 squares (2 ounces) unsweetened
  chocolate
2 tablespoons butter or margarine
2/3 cup packed light brown sugar
2/3 cup dark corn syrup
3 large eggs, lightly beaten
1 teaspoon vanilla extract
11/2 cups pecans (6 ounces),
  coarsely chopped

1. Preheat oven to 350°F. Line 13" by 9" baking pan with foil, extending foil over rim.

2. Prepare Crust: In medium bowl, with mixer at medium speed, beat butter and confectioners' sugar until combined. Reduce speed to low; beat in flour until combined. With lightly floured hand, press dough into bottom and 1 inch up side of prepared pan. Line crust with foil; fill with pie weights or dry beans. Bake until lightly golden, 15 to 20 minutes. Cool on wire rack to room temperature; remove foil and weights.

3. Meanwhile, prepare Filling: In 3-quart saucepan, melt semisweet and unsweetened chocolates and butter over low heat, stirring frequently, until smooth. Remove from heat; cool to lukewarm. With rubber spatula, stir in brown sugar and corn syrup until smooth. Stir in eggs, vanilla, and pecans.

4. Pour filling over cooled crust. Bake until set, about 30 minutes. Cool completely in pan on rack.

5. When cool, transfer pastry with foil to cutting board; peel away foil from sides. Cut lengthwise into 4 strips, then cut each strip crosswise into 8 pieces.

Each bar: About 177 calories, 2g protein, 20g carbohydrate, 10g total fat (4g saturated), 34mg cholesterol, 70mg sodium.

Chocolate Swirl Peanut Butter Blondies

It is hard to resist the combination of peanut butter and chocolate. To make this confection even more irresistible, chocolate chips are sprinkled on top.

PREP: 20 MINUTES   BAKE: 25 MINUTES   MAKES 24 BLONDIES

2 1/2 cups all-purpose flour
1 1/2 teaspoons baking powder
1/2 teaspoon salt
3 squares (3 ounces) semisweet chocolate, chopped
1 square (1 ounce) unsweetened chocolate, chopped
1 cup creamy peanut butter

1/2 cup butter or margarine (1 stick), softened
1 3/4 cups packed light brown sugar
3 large eggs
2 teaspoons vanilla extract
1 package (6 ounces) semisweet chocolate chips (1 cup)

1. Preheat oven to 350°F. In medium bowl, combine flour, baking powder, and salt. In heavy 1-quart saucepan, melt semisweet and unsweetened chocolates over low heat, stirring frequently, until smooth.

2. In large bowl, with mixer at medium speed, beat peanut butter, butter, and brown sugar until light and fluffy, about 2 minutes. Add eggs and vanilla; beat until blended. Reduce speed to low; beat in flour mixture just until blended (dough will be stiff).

3. Place one-third of dough (about 1 3/4 cups) in separate large bowl. Stir in melted chocolate until blended; stir in 3/4 cup chocolate chips.

4. With hand, pat half of remaining plain peanut butter dough onto bottom of ungreased 13" by 9" baking pan to form thin layer. In random pattern, drop chocolate dough and remaining plain peanut butter dough on top of peanut butter layer; lightly pat. Sprinkle remaining 1/4 cup chocolate chips on top.

5. Bake until toothpick inserted in center comes out clean, 25 to 30 minutes. Cool completely in pan on wire rack.

6. When cool, cut blondie lengthwise into 4 strips, then cut each strip crosswise into 6 pieces. Makes 24 blondies.

Each blondie: About 273 calories, 6g protein, 34g carbohydrate, 14g total fat (6g saturated), 37mg cholesterol, 184mg sodium.

Mississippi Mud Bars

Bake up to two weeks ahead, cut, wrap, and freeze. They're terrific straight from the freezer, too!

PREP: 20 MINUTES PLUS COOLING   BAKE: 35 MINUTES
MAKES 32 BARS

MUD CAKE
3/4 cup butter or margarine
   (1 1/2 sticks)
1 3/4 cups sugar
3/4 cup unsweetened cocoa
4 large eggs
2 teaspoons vanilla extract
1/2 teaspoon salt
1 1/2 cups all-purpose flour
1/2 cup pecans, chopped
1/2 cup flaked, sweetened coconut
3 cups miniature marshmallows

FUDGE TOPPING
5 tablespoons butter or margarine
1 square (1 ounce) unsweetened
   chocolate
1/3 cup unsweetened cocoa
1/8 teaspoon salt
1/4 cup evaporated milk
   (not sweetened condensed milk)
   or heavy or whipping cream
1 teaspoon vanilla extract
1 cup confectioners' sugar
1/2 cup pecans, coarsely broken
1/4 cup flaked sweetened coconut

1. Preheat oven to 350°F. Grease and flour 13" by 9" baking pan.

2. Prepare Mud Cake: In 3-quart saucepan, melt butter over low heat. With wire whisk, stir in granulated sugar and cocoa. Add eggs, one at a time. Beat in vanilla and salt until well blended. Remove from heat. With wooden spoon, stir flour mixture into cocoa mixture just until blended. Stir in pecans and coconut. Spread batter evenly in prepared pan (batter will be thick).

3. Bake 25 minutes. Remove from oven. Sprinkle marshmallows in even layer on top of cake. Return cake to oven and bake until marshmallows are puffed and golden, about 10 minutes longer. Cool completely in pan on wire rack.

4. When cake is cool, prepare Fudge Topping: In 2-quart saucepan, melt butter and chocolate over low heat, stirring frequently, until smooth. With wire whisk, stir in cocoa and salt until smooth. Stir in evaporated milk and vanilla (mixture will be thick); beat in confectioners' sugar until smooth and blended. Pour hot topping over cooled cake.

5. Cool fudge-topped cake 20 minutes; sprinkle with pecans and coconut. Cover pan and store at room temperature or freeze up to 2 weeks. Serve chilled or at room temperature. To serve, cut cake lengthwise into 4 strips, then cut each strip crosswise into 8 pieces.

Each bar: About 205 calories, 3g protein, 27g carbohydrate, 11g total fat (4g saturated), 39mg cholesterol, 126mg sodium.

Apricot Fudgies

Nestlé introduced the first American white chocolate bar in 1987. It quickly became available in supermarkets across the country, and we were infatuated with it—in sauces, cheesecakes, and chunky cookies. In fact, anything chocolaty—rich, light, or dark—was a big hit.

PREP: 30 MINUTES PLUS COOLING   BAKE: 13 MINUTES PER BATCH
MAKES 36 COOKIES

1/4 cup all-purpose flour
1/4 cup unsweetened cocoa
1/2 teaspoon baking powder
1/4 teaspoon salt
8 squares (8 ounces) semisweet chocolate, coarsely chopped
6 tablespoons butter or margarine, cut into pieces
3/4 cup sugar

2 teaspoons vanilla extract
2 large eggs
6 ounces white chocolate, Swiss confectionery bar, or white baking bar, coarsely chopped
1 cup dried apricot halves (about 8 ounces), coarsely chopped

1. Preheat oven to 350°F. In small bowl, combine flour, cocoa, baking powder, and salt.

2. In 3-quart saucepan, melt semisweet chocolate and butter over low heat, stirring frequently, until smooth. Remove from heat; with wire whisk, stir in sugar and vanilla until blended. Whisk in eggs, one at a time, until mixture is smooth. With wooden spoon, stir flour mixture into chocolate mixture until combined. Add white chocolate and apricots; stir just until evenly mixed (dough will be loose and sticky).

3. Drop dough by rounded tablespoons, 1½ inches apart, onto ungreased large cookie sheet. Bake until tops of cookies are set, 13 to 15 minutes. Cool 30 seconds on cookie sheet. With wide spatula, transfer cookies to wire rack to cool completely. Repeat with remaining dough.

Each cookie: About 110 calories, 2g protein, 14g carbohydrate, 6g total fat (4g saturated), 18mg cholesterol, 49mg sodium.

Double-Chocolate Chunk Cookies

We love these cookies for the bigger-than-usual chunks of chocolate they contain. You can use packaged chocolate chunks as we did here or purchase high-quality chocolate and cut it up.

PREP: 30 MINUTES   BAKE: 25 MINUTES PER BATCH
MAKES 18 COOKIES

2 cups all-purpose flour
1 teaspoon baking soda
1/2 teaspoon salt
1 package (12 ounces) semisweet chocolate chunks or 12 ounces coarsely chopped semisweet chocolate (2 cups)
1 cup butter or margarine (2 sticks), softened

2/3 cup packed light brown sugar
1/3 cup granulated sugar
2 teaspoons vanilla extract
1 large egg
2 cups walnuts (8 ounces), coarsely chopped

1. Preheat oven to 350°F. In medium bowl, combine flour, baking soda, and salt.

2. In heavy 1-quart saucepan, melt 1 cup chocolate chunks over low heat, stirring frequently, until smooth. Remove from heat; cool to room temperature.

3. In large bowl, with mixer at low speed, beat butter, brown and granulated sugars, and vanilla until crumbly. Add melted chocolate and egg; beat until well blended, occasionally scraping bowl with rubber spatula. With wooden spoon, stir in flour mixture until blended. Stir in walnuts and remaining chocolate chunks.

4. Drop dough by level 1/4 cups, about 3 inches apart, on ungreased large cookie sheet. Bake cookies until edges are set but centers are still soft, 25 to 30 minutes. With wide spatula, transfer cookies to wire racks to cool completely.

5. Repeat with remaining dough.

Each serving: About 360 calories, 5g protein, 37g carbohydrate, 24g total fat (3g saturated), 12mg cholesterol, 255mg sodium.

Triple-Chocolate Chubbies

Can the classic chocolate chip cookie be improved upon? The answer is "yes" if your definition of improvement is "more chocolate." There's melted chocolate as well as cocoa in the dough, and semisweet chocolate chips are dotted throughout these big cookies. If you don't want to use both pecans and walnuts, use 1 cup of either one.

PREP: 25 MINUTES   BAKE: 14 MINUTES PER BATCH
MAKES ABOUT 24 COOKIES

1/4 cup all-purpose flour
1/4 cup unsweetened cocoa
1/2 teaspoon baking powder
1/4 teaspoon salt
8 squares (8 ounces) semisweet chocolate, chopped
6 tablespoons butter or margarine, cut into pieces

1 cup sugar
2 teaspoons vanilla extract
2 large eggs
1 package (6 ounces) semisweet chocolate chips (1 cup)
1/2 cup pecans, chopped
1/2 cup walnuts, chopped

1. Preheat oven to 350°F. In small bowl, combine flour, cocoa, baking powder, and salt.
2. In 3-quart saucepan, melt chocolate and butter over low heat, stirring frequently, until smooth. Pour into large bowl; cool to lukewarm. Stir in sugar and vanilla until blended. Stir in eggs, one at a time, until well blended. Add flour mixture; stir until combined (batter will be thin). Stir in chocolate chips, pecans, and walnuts.
3. Drop batter by heaping tablespoons, 1 1/2 inches apart, on ungreased large cookie sheet. Bake until set, about 14 minutes. Cool on cookie sheet on wire rack 2 minutes. With wide spatula, carefully transfer cookies to racks to cool completely.
4. Repeat with remaining dough.

Each cookie: About 180 calories, 2g protein, 21g carbohydrate, 11g total fat (5g saturated), 26mg cholesterol, 70mg sodium.

Chocolate Wows

After one bite of these decadent cookies, you will understand why we call them "Wows."

PREP: 20 MINUTES PLUS COOLING   BAKE: 13 MINUTES PER BATCH
MAKES ABOUT 48 COOKIES

1/3 cup all-purpose flour
1/4 cup unsweetened cocoa
1 teaspoon baking powder
1/4 teaspoon salt
8 squares (6 ounces) semisweet
    chocolate, chopped
1/2 cup butter or margarine (1 stick)

3/4 cup sugar
2 large eggs
11/2 teaspoons vanilla extract
2 cups pecans (8 ounces), chopped
1 package (6 ounces) semisweet
    chocolate chips (1 cup)

1. Preheat oven to 325°F. Grease two large cookie sheets. In small bowl, combine flour, cocoa, baking powder, and salt.
2. In heavy 2-quart saucepan, melt chocolate and butter over low heat, stirring frequently, until smooth. Remove from heat; cool.
3. In large bowl, with mixer at medium speed, beat sugar and eggs until light and lemon colored, about 2 minutes, frequently scraping bowl with rubber spatula. Reduce speed to low. Add cooled chocolate mixture, flour mixture, and vanilla; beat just until blended. Increase speed to medium; beat 2 minutes. With wooden spoon, stir in pecans and chocolate chips.
4. Drop batter by rounded teaspoons, 2 inches apart, on prepared cookie sheets. With small metal spatula, spread batter into 2-inch rounds. Bake until tops are shiny and cracked, 13 to 15 minutes, rotating cookie sheets between upper and lower oven racks halfway through baking. Cool 10 minutes on cookie sheet on wire racks. With wide spatula, transfer cookies to racks to cool completely.
5. Repeat with remaining batter.

Each cookie: About 102 calories, 1g protein, 9g carbohydrate, 7g total fat (3g saturated), 14mg cholesterol, 45mg sodium.

Rich Chocolate-Cherry Cookies

Former Food Associate Lori Perlmutter has enjoyed these cookies for years, thanks to her mother-in-law, Clare Conforti. According to Lori, every holiday season her family anxiously awaited the delivery of Mrs. Conforti's heavenly cookies. They eventually became a tradition in the Perlmutter family also.

PREP: 30 MINUTES PLUS COOLING   BAKE: 13 MINUTES PER BATCH
MAKES 36 COOKIES

1/4 cup all-purpose flour
1/4 cup unsweetened cocoa
1/2 teaspoon baking powder
1/4 teaspoon salt
8 squares (8 ounces) semisweet
   chocolate, coarsely chopped
6 tablespoons butter or margarine,
   cut into pieces

3/4 cup sugar
2 teaspoons vanilla extract
2 large eggs
1 package (6 ounces) semisweet
   chocolate chips (1 cup)
1 cup dried tart cherries

1. Preheat oven to 350°F. In large bowl, combine flour, cocoa, baking powder, and salt.

2. In 3-quart saucepan, melt chocolate and butter over low heat, stirring frequently, until smooth. Remove from heat; with wire whisk, stir in sugar and vanilla until blended. Whisk in eggs, one at a time, until blended. With wooden spoon, stir in flour mixture. Add chocolate chips and cherries; stir just until evenly mixed.

3. Drop dough by rounded tablespoons, 1½ inches apart, onto ungreased large cookie sheet. Bake until tops of cookies are set, 13 to 15 minutes. Cool on cookie sheet on wire rack 1 minute. With wide spatula, transfer cookies to wire racks to cool completely.

4. Repeat with remaining dough.

Each serving: About 105 calories, 1g protein, 16g carbohydrate, 5g total fat (2g saturated), 17mg cholesterol, 49g sodium.

Double Chocolate-Cherry Drops

The sublte tartness of the cherries provides a delicious contrast to the double dose of rich chocolate from semisweet chunks and cocoa.

PREP: 25 MINUTES   BAKE: 10 MINUTES PER BATCH   MAKES 60 COOKIES

1³/4 cups all-purpose flour
³/4 cup unsweetened cocoa
1/4 teaspoon salt
1 cup butter or margarine (2 sticks), softened
1 cup sugar
1/4 cup light corn syrup

1 large egg
2 teaspoons vanilla extract
1 package (8 ounces) semisweet-chocolate squares or 8 ounces white chocolate, cut into 1/2-inch pieces
1 cup dried tart cherries

1. Preheat oven to 350°F. In medium bowl, combine flour, cocoa, and salt.
2. In large bowl, with mixer at medium speed, beat butter and sugar until creamy, occasionally scraping bowl with rubber spatula. Beat in corn syrup, egg, and vanilla until well mixed. Reduce speed to low. Gradually add flour mixture; beat just until blended, occasionally scraping bowl. With wooden spoon, stir in chocolate and cherries.
3. Drop cookies by rounded teaspoons, 2 inches apart, onto ungreased cookie sheet. Bake until tops are just firm, 10 to 11 minutes. With wide spatula, transfer cookies to wire racks to cool completely.
4. Repeat with remaining dough.

Each serving: About 84 calories, 1g protein, 11g carbohydrate, 5g total fat (3g saturated), 12mg cholesterol, 50mg sodium.

Whoopie Pies

You may remember these yummy treats from your childhood: soft, cakelike cookies that are sandwiched with fluffy marshallow crème.

PREP: 30 MINUTES PLUS COOLING   BAKE: 12 MINUTES
MAKES 12 WHOOPIE PIES

2 cups all-purpose flour	6 tablespoons butter or margarine,
1 cup sugar	melted
1/2 cup unsweetened cocoa	1 large egg
1 teaspoon baking soda	1 teaspoon vanilla extract
1/4 teaspoon salt	Marshmallow Crème Filling (below)
3/4 cup milk	

1. Preheat oven to 350°F. Grease 2 large cookie sheets.

2. In large bowl, with wooden spoon, combine flour, sugar, cocoa, baking soda, and salt. Add milk, butter, egg, and vanilla; stir until smooth.

3. Drop 12 heaping tablespoons batter, 2 inches apart, on each prepared cookie sheet.

4. Bake until puffy and toothpick inserted in center comes out clean, 12 to 14 minutes, rotating cookie sheets between upper and lower racks halfway through baking time. With wide spatula, transfer cookies to wire racks to cool completely.

5. When cool, prepare Marshmallow Crème Filling. Spread 1 rounded tablespoon filling over flat side of 12 cookies. Top with remaining cookies, flat side down, to make 12 sandwiches.

Marshmallow Crème Filling: In large bowl, with mixer at medium speed, beat **6 tablespoons butter or margarine,** slightly softened, until creamy. With mixer at low speed, gradually beat in **1 cup confectioners' sugar** until blended. Beat in **1 jar (7 to 7 1/2-ounces) marshmallow crème** (about 1 1/2 cups) and **1 teaspoon vanilla extract** until well combined.

Each whoopie pie: About 360 calories, 4g protein, 60g carbohydrate, 13g total fat (8g saturated), 51mg cholesterol, 289mg sodium.

No-Bake Chocolate Crackles

If you love Rice Krispies, you'll love these easy-to-prepare no-bake cookies, which are ideal for children's parties. Stack them on a platter or place them in whimsical paper cups that are found in cookware and cake-decorating stores.

PREP: 10 MINUTES PLUS CHILLING   MAKES 9 COOKIES

3 squares (3 ounces) semisweet chocolate
2 cups crispy rice cereal

2 rectangular graham crackers, broken into small pieces

1. Line cookie sheet with waxed paper. In 2-quart microwave-safe bowl, heat chocolate in microwave oven on High 1 to 1 1/2 minutes, until melted, stirring once. Add cereal and crackers; stir until coated.

2. Drop mixture by 1/3 cups onto prepared cookie sheet. With fingertips, shape mixture to form rounded mounds if necessary. Refrigerate cookies until set, about 30 minutes.

Each cookie: About 85 calories, 1g protein, 14g carbohydrate, 3g total fat (2g saturated), 0mg cholesterol, 65mg sodium.

Chocolate-Espresso Walnut Clusters

Here is a real easy recipe to put together. All of the ingredients (except for the walnuts) are mixed together in a bowl and dropped in mounds onto a cookie sheet. The instant espresso-coffee powder adds a healthy dose of coffee flavor. It is found in supermarkets in the coffee aisle.

PREP: 30 MINUTES   BAKE: 15 MINUTES PER BATCH
MAKES 36 COOKIES

1 cup all-purpose flour
1 cup sugar
1 tablespoon instant espresso-coffee powder
1 teaspoon salt
1/2 teaspoon baking powder
3 squares (3 ounces) unsweetened chocolate, melted

1/2 cup butter or margarine (1 stick), softened
2 large eggs
2 teaspoons vanilla extract
4 cups walnuts (about 16 ounces), coarsely broken

1. Preheat oven to 350°F. In large bowl, combine flour, sugar, coffee powder, salt, and baking powder. Add melted chocolate, butter, eggs, and vanilla. With mixer at low speed, beat until well mixed, occasionally scraping bowl with rubber spatula. With wooden spoon, stir in walnuts.
2. Drop dough by rounded tablespoons, 1 inch apart, onto ungreased large cookie sheet. Bake until set, about 15 minutes. With wide metal spatula, transfer to wire rack to cool.
3. Repeat with remaining dough.

Each cookie: About 160 calories, 3g protein, 11g carbohydrate, 12g total fat (3g saturated), 19mg cholesterol, 92mg sodium.

Chocolate-Hazelnut Macaroons

Chocolate plus hazelnut equals *gianduia*—a flavor you may have encountered in fine Italian chocolates. These macaroons are a chocolate variation of an Italian recipe called *brutti ma buoni* (ugly but good)—a reference to the fact that the cookies are a bit lumpy and irregular in shape, though absolutely delicious.

PREP: 30 MINUTES   BAKE: 10 MINUTES PER BATCH
MAKES ABOUT 30 COOKIES

1 cup hazelnuts (filberts; 4 ounces)
1 cup sugar
1/4 cup unsweetened cocoa
1 square (1 ounce) unsweetened chocolate, chopped

1/8 teaspoon salt
2 large egg whites
1 teaspoon vanilla extract

1. Preheat oven to 350°F. Line two large cookie sheets with foil.

2. Place hazelnuts in small shallow baking pan. Bake until toasted, about 15 minutes. Wrap hot hazelnuts in clean kitchen towel. Using the towel, roll hazelnuts back and forth to remove most of skins. Cool completely.

3. In food processor with knife blade attached, process cooled hazelnuts, sugar, cocoa, chocolate, and salt until nuts and chocolate are finely ground. Add egg whites and vanilla; process until well blended.

4. Drop dough by rounded teaspoons, using another spoon to help release batter, 2 inches apart, on prepared cookie sheets. Bake until tops feel firm when pressed lightly, about 10 minutes, rotating sheets between upper and lower racks halfway through baking. Cool completely on cookie sheets on wire racks.

5. Repeat with remaining cookie dough.

Each cookie: About 60 calories, 1g protein, 8g carbohydrate, 3g total fat (1g saturated), 0 mg cholesterol, 15mg sodium.

Chocolate Macaroons

Macaroons have the most tempting texture: crisp on the outside and soft and chewy on the inside. These almond-chocolate macaroons are made even more fabulous, as they are sandwiched with a heavenly chocolate and whipped cream filling.

PREP: 20 MINUTES PLUS COOLING   BAKE: 13 MINUTES PER BATCH
MAKES ABOUT 36 COOKIES

1 cup blanched slivered almonds
1 cup sugar
2 tablespoons unsweetened cocoa
pinch salt
1/3 cup egg whites
2 squares (2 ounces) unsweetened
    chocolate, melted and cooled
1/2 teaspoon vanilla extract

CHOCOLATE FILLING
1/4 cup heavy or whipping cream
1 1/2 teaspoons sugar
1 teaspoon butter or margarine
3 ounces bittersweet chocolate or
    3 squares (3 ounces) semisweet
    chocolate, chopped
1/4 teaspoon vanilla extract

1. Preheat oven to 350°F. Line 2 large cookie sheets with parchment paper.

2. In food processor with knife blade attached, combine almonds, sugar, cocoa, and salt; process until almonds are ground to a powder. Add egg whites, melted chocolate, and vanilla; process until a paste is formed.

3. Transfer batter to large pastry bag fitted with 3/4-inch round tip. Pipe batter into 1-inch mounds, 2 inches apart, on prepared cookie sheets. Bake until almost firm, 13 to 14 minutes. Cool macaroons 1 minute on cookie sheets on wire racks. With wide spatula, carefully transfer macaroons to racks to cool completely.

4. Prepare Chocolate Filling: In 1-quart saucepan, combine cream, sugar, and butter; heat to boiling over medium-high heat. Remove from heat. Add chocolate to cream mixture; stir until melted and smooth. Stir in vanilla. Pour into small shallow bowl; refrigerate until firm and spreadable, at least 1 hour.

5. Turn half of macaroons, flat bottoms facing up. With small metal spatula, spread scant 2 teaspoons chocolate filling on macaroons. Place remaining macaroons on top to make sandwiches.

Each cookie: About 68 calories, 1g protein, 8g carbohydrate, 4g total fat (2g saturated), 3mg cholesterol, 10mg sodium.

Chocolate Crinkles

Rolling the dough in confectioners' sugar produces a snowy-looking finish appropriate for the winter holidays. For a change, roll the dough in granulated sugar, which gives the cookies a crackly-shiny coat.

PREP: 25 MINUTES PLUS CHILLING   BAKE: 8 MINUTES PER BATCH
MAKES ABOUT 96 COOKIES

1³/₄ cups all-purpose flour
1/₂ cup unsweetened cocoa
1 teaspoon baking soda
1/₂ teaspoon baking powder
1/₄ teaspoon salt
1/₂ cup butter or margarine (1 stick), softened

1¹/₄ cups granulated sugar
2 tablespoons light corn syrup
2 squares (2 ounces) unsweetened chocolate, melted and cooled
2 large eggs
2 teaspoons vanilla extract
1/₂ cup confectioners' sugar

1. In large bowl, combine flour, cocoa, baking soda, baking powder, and salt.

2. In large bowl, with mixer at medium speed, beat butter, granulated sugar, and corn syrup until combined. Reduce speed to low; beat in chocolate, eggs, and vanilla until well blended. Beat in flour mixture until combined, occasionally scraping bowl with rubber spatula. Cover dough; refrigerate until firm, about 1 hour.

3. Preheat oven to 350°F. Place confectioners' sugar in shallow bowl. Shape dough into 1-inch balls; roll in confectioners' sugar to coat. Place cookies, 1 inch apart, on ungreased large cookie sheet. Bake 8 minutes. With wide spatula, transfer cookies to wire racks to cool completely.

4. Repeat with remaining dough and confectioners' sugar.

Each cookie: About 35 calories, 1g protein, 6g carbohydrate, 1g total fat (1g saturated), 7mg cholesterol, 35mg sodium.

Chocolate-Coconut Bites

You get chocolate three ways in these tempting bites: melted chocolate, cocoa, and chocolate chips. To make quick work of shaping the dough into balls, use a very small ice-cream scoop, which is available in cookware stores.

PREP: 30 MINUTES PLUS CHILLING AND COOLING
BAKE: 12 MINUTES PER BATCH
MAKES 48 COOKIES

8 squares (8 ounces) semisweet
   chocolate, chopped
6 tablespoons butter or margarine,
   cut into pieces
1/3 cup all-purpose flour
1/4 cup unsweetened cocoa
1/2 teaspoon baking powder

1/4 teaspoon salt
3/4 cup sugar
2 teaspoons vanilla extract
2 large eggs
1 package (6 ounces) semisweet
   chocolate chips (1 cup)
1 cup sweetened flaked coconut

1. In 1-quart saucepan, melt chocolate and butter over low heat, stirring frequently, until smooth. Pour chocolate mixture into large bowl; cool to lukewarm, about 10 minutes.

2. Meanwhile, in small bowl, combine, flour, cocoa, baking powder, and salt.

3. Stir sugar and vanilla into chocolate mixture until blended. Add eggs, one at a time, stirring until blended. Add flour mixture, chocolate chips, and coconut; stir until combined. Cover with plastic wrap; refrigerate until firm, about 1 hour.

4. Meanwhile, preheat oven to 350°F. Shape dough into 1 1/2-inch balls and place, 2 inches apart, on ungreased large cookie sheet. Bake until set, 12 to 14 minutes. Cool on cookie sheet on wire rack 2 minutes. With wide spatula, carefully transfer cookies to rack to cool completely. Clean edge of spatula after each batch, if necessary, for easier removal of cookies from cookie sheet.

5. Repeat with remaining dough.

Each cookie: About 85 calories, 1g protein, 10g carbohydrate, 5g total fat (3g saturated), 13mg cholesterol, 40mg sodium.

Cocoa Wedding Cakes

These cookies are a delicious twist on wedding cookies (*pastelitos de boda*), the traditional sweet served at weddings in Mexico. Their texture is reminiscent of pecan shortbread cookies, which no doubt accounts for their popularity. Our version contains cocoa and chocolate chips.

PREP: 45 MINUTES PLUS COOLING BAKE: 16 MINUTES PER BATCH
MAKES 54 COOKIES

1 cup pecans (4 ounces)
1 3/4 cups confectioners' sugar
1 cup cold butter (2 sticks), cut into
  pieces (do not use margarine)
1 teaspoon vanilla extract

1 3/4 cups all-purpose flour
1/3 cup unsweetened cocoa
1/3 cup semisweet-chocolate
  mini chips

1. Preheat oven to 325°F.
2. In food processor with knife blade attached, combine pecans and 1/2 cup confectioners' sugar; pulse until pecans are finely ground. Add butter and vanilla; process until smooth, occasionally scraping bowl with rubber spatula. Add flour and cocoa; pulse until evenly mixed. Add chocolate chips; pulse until just combined.
3. With floured hands, roll dough into 1-inch balls. Place balls, 1 inch apart, on ungreased large cookie sheet. Bake until bottoms are lightly browned, 16 to 18 minutes. With wide spatula, transfer cookies to wire racks to cool slightly.
4. Sift remaining 1 1/4 cups confectioners' sugar onto waxed paper. While cookies are still warm, roll in sugar to coat; return to rack to cool completely. When cool, gently roll cookies in sugar again until evenly coated.
5. Repeat with remaining dough and sugar.

Each serving: About 80 calories, 1g protein, 8g carbohydrate, 6g total fat (3g saturated), 10mg cholesterol, 35mg sodium.

Chocolate-Mint Sandwiches

Reminiscent of a favorite Girl Scout cookie, these are popular with grownups and children.

PREP: 40 MINUTES PLUS COOLING   BAKE: 12 MINUTES PER BATCH
MAKES 54 COOKIES

2 cups all-purpose flour
1/2 cup plus 1/3 cup sugar
2 teaspoons baking soda
1/4 teaspoon salt
6 squares (6 ounces) semisweet chocolate, melted and cooled

10 tablespoons butter or margarine (1 1/4 sticks), softened
1/4 cup light or dark corn syrup
2 large eggs
2 bags (13 ounces each) chocolate-covered mint patties (about 54)

1. Preheat oven to 350°F. In large bowl, combine flour, 1/2 cup sugar, baking soda, and salt. Add melted chocolate, butter, corn syrup, and eggs. With mixer at low speed, beat until blended. Increase speed to medium; beat until well mixed, frequently scraping bowl with rubber spatula.

2. Shape dough by rounded teaspoons into balls. Roll balls in remaining 1/3 cup sugar until coated. Place balls, 2 inches apart, on ungreased large cookie sheet. Bake until set, 12 to 14 minutes. Immediately turn half of cookies over on cookie sheet. While still hot, place chocolate-covered mint patty on each inverted cookie; quickly top with remaining cookies, top side up. With wide spatula, transfer sandwich cookies to wire racks to cool 1 minute; press cookies together slightly so mint patty spreads to cookie edges as it melts. Cool cookies completely on racks.

3. Repeat with remaining dough balls, sugar, and mint patties.

Each cookie: About 120 calories, 1g protein, 20g carbohydrate, 4g total fat (3g saturated), 47mg cholesterol, 88mg sodium.

Mostaccioli

The Italian word *mostaccioli* comes from the Latin word for cookies, *mustaceum*. The ancient Romans made them from ground almonds, flour, grape must, and spices. They were usually served at weddings and other feasts. Modern-day versions often contain cocoa, as does our excellent rendition.

PREP: 45 MINUTES PLUS COOLING   BAKE: 7 MINUTES PER BATCH
MAKES 60 COOKIES

COOKIES
2 cups all-purpose flour
1/2 cup unsweetened cocoa
1 1/2 teaspoons baking powder
1 teaspoon ground cinnamon
1/4 teaspoon ground cloves
1/4 teaspoon salt
1/2 cup butter or margarine (1 stick), softened

3/4 cup granulated sugar
1 large egg
1/2 cup milk

CHOCOLATE GLAZE
3 tablespoons unsweetened cocoa
1/4 cup boiling water
1 1/4 cups confectioners' sugar
white candy decors

1. Prepare Cookies: Preheat oven to 400°F. In medium bowl, combine flour, cocoa, baking powder, cinnamon, cloves, and salt.

2. In large bowl, with mixer at low speed, beat butter and granulated sugar until blended, occasionally scraping bowl with rubber spatula. Increase speed to high; beat until light and creamy. Reduce speed to low; beat in egg. Alternately beat in flour mixture and milk, beginning and ending with flour mixture, just until combined, occasionally scraping bowl.

3. With cocoa-dusted hands, roll dough into 1-inch balls. Place balls, 2 inches apart, on ungreased large cookie sheet. Bake until puffed (dry looking, and slightly cracked), 7 to 9 minutes. With wide spatula, transfer cookies to wire racks to cool. Repeat with remaining dough.

4. When cookies are cool, prepare Chocolate Glaze: In medium bowl, with wire whisk or fork, stir cocoa into water until smooth. Gradually stir in confectioners' sugar until blended. Dip top of each cookie into glaze. Place cookies on wire racks set over waxed paper to catch any drips. Immediately sprinkle cookies with decors. Allow glaze to set, about 20 minutes.

Each cookie: About 55 calories, 1g protein, 9g carbohydrate, 2g total fat (1g saturated), 8mg cholesterol, 40mg sodium.

Chocolate Sambuca Cookies

A close friend shared this recipe with *GH* reader Leslie Husted several years ago. Her family looks forward to nibbling on these every year at holiday time, and she makes batches to give as gifts.

PREP: 30 MINUTES PLUS CHILLING AND COOLING
BAKE: 10 MINUTES PER BATCH   MAKES 48 COOKIES

12 squares (12 ounces) semisweet chocolate
4 tablespoons butter or margarine
1 cup granulated sugar
1/3 cup sambuca (anise-flavored liqueur)
3 large eggs

1 cup whole blanched almonds (4 ounces), finely ground
2/3 cup all-purpose flour
3/4 teaspoon baking soda
1/3 cup confectioners' sugar

1. In 2-quart saucepan, melt chocolate and butter over low heat, stirring frequently, until smooth. Remove from heat; cool slightly.

2. In medium bowl, with wire whisk, mix 1/2 cup sugar, sambuca, and eggs; stir in chocolate mixture until blended.

3. With wooden spoon, stir ground almonds, flour, and baking soda into chocolate mixture until combined (dough will be very soft). Cover bowl with plastic wrap; refrigerate until firm, at least 4 hours or up to overnight.

4. Preheat oven to 350°F. In small bowl, combine confectioners' sugar with remaining 1/2 cup granulated sugar. With lightly floured hands, roll rounded tablespoons dough into balls; roll in sugar mixture to coat. Place balls, about 2 inches apart, on ungreased large cookie sheet. Bake until cookies are just set and look puffed and cracked, 10 to 12 minutes. Cool 1 minute on cookie sheet on wire rack. With wide spatula, transfer cookies to racks to cool completely.

5. Repeat with remaining dough and sugar mixture.

Each cookie: About 85 calories, 2g protein, 12g carbohydrate, 4g total fat (1g saturated), 16mg cholesterol, 17mg sodium.

Chocolate Roll-Out Cookies

Use these cocoa-rich treats to decorate your Christmas tree when the holidays roll around. Before they are baked, use a straw or bamboo skewer to make a hole at the top of each one.

PREP: 45 MINUTES PLUS COOLING AND DECORATING
BAKE: 12 MINUTES PER BATCH   MAKES 36 COOKIES

1 1/2 cups all-purpose flour
1/2 cup unsweetened cocoa
1 teaspoon baking powder
1/2 teaspoon salt
3/4 cup butter or margarine
  (1 1/2 sticks), softened

2/3 cup sugar
1 large egg
2 tablespoons water
1 1/2 teaspoons vanilla extract

1. Preheat oven to 350°F. Grease and flour 2 large cookie sheets. In medium bowl, combine flour, cocoa, baking powder, and salt.

2. In large bowl with mixer at low speed, beat butter and sugar until blended. Increase speed to high; beat until light and creamy, about 2 minutes. Reduce speed to low. Add flour mixture, egg, water, and vanilla; beat until blended.

3. On lightly floured surface, with floured rolling pin, roll dough slightly less than 1/4 inch thick. With floured 3- to 4-inch holiday cookie cutters, cut dough into as many cookies as possible; reserve trimmings. Place cookies, 1/2 inch apart, on prepared cookie sheets.

4. Bake until brown, 12 to 15 minutes, rotating cookie sheets between upper and lower racks halfway through baking time. With wide spatula, transfer cookies to wire racks to cool.

5. Repeat with remaining dough and trimmings.

Each cookie: About 70 calories, 1g protein, 8g carbohydrate, 4g total fat (4g saturated), 27mg cholesterol, 71mg sodium.

Double-Chocolate Biscotti

These classic crunchy Italian cookies are delectable with a mug of freshly brewed coffee or a glass of ice-cold milk.

PREP: 30 MINUTES PLUS COOLING   BAKE: 50 MINUTES
MAKES 36 BISCOTTI

2¹/₂ cups all-purpose flour
³/₄ cup unsweetened cocoa
1 tablespoon baking powder
¹/₂ teaspoon salt
¹/₂ cup butter or margarine
  (1 stick), softened
1¹/₃ cups sugar
3 large eggs

2 squares (2 ounces) semisweet
  chocolate, melted
1 teaspoon instant espresso-coffee
  powder
1 teaspoon hot water
³/₄ cup semisweet-chocolate
  mini chips

1. Preheat oven to 350°F. Grease and flour large cookie sheet. In large bowl combine flour, cocoa, baking powder, and salt.

2. In another large bowl, with mixer at medium speed, beat butter and sugar until creamy. Reduce speed to low. Add eggs, one at a time, beating well after each addition. Add melted chocolate; beat until well combined.

3. In cup, dissolve espresso-coffee powder in hot water; beat into chocolate mixture. Add flour mixture; beat just until blended. With hands, knead in chocolate chips until combined.

4. On floured surface, with floured hands, divide dough in half. Shape each piece of dough into 12" by 3" log. With pastry brush, brush off excess flour. Place logs, 3 inches apart, on cookie sheet. Bake 30 minutes. Cool logs on cookie sheet on wire rack 10 minutes.

5. Transfer 1 log to cutting board. With serrated knife, cut log crosswise on diagonal into ³/₄-inch-thick slices. Repeat with remaining log. Place slices, cut side down, on same cookie sheet. Bake 20 to 25 minutes to dry biscotti. With wide spatula, transfer biscotti to wire racks to cool completely. (Biscotti will harden as they cool.)

Each biscotti: About 115 calories, 2g protein, 19g carbohydrate, 4g total fat (2g saturated), 25mg cholesterol, 97mg sodium.

Chocolate–Dried Cherry Biscotti

Prepare as directed but substitute **3/4 cup dried tart cherries,** coarsely chopped, for chocolate chips.

Each biscotti: About 83 calories, 1g protein, 14g carbohydrate, 3g total fat (2g saturated), 17mg cholesterol, 79mg sodium.

Chocolate Biscotti

A generous recipe that makes dozens of delicious biscotti. Store some in freezer-safe ziptight plastic bags for up to several months.

PREP: 45 MINUTES PLUS COOLING AND CHILLING   BAKE: 45 MINUTES
MAKES 84 BISCOTTI

2 1/2 cups all-purpose flour
1 cup unsweetened cocoa
1 tablespoon baking powder
1 teaspoon instant-coffee granules
1/2 teaspoon salt
1 cup butter or margarine (2 sticks), softened

1 cup sugar
1 teaspoon vanilla extract
4 large eggs
8 squares (8 ounces) semisweet chocolate
1/4 cup sliced almonds, toasted (page 97)

1. Preheat oven to 350°F. In medium bowl, combine 1 cup flour, cocoa, baking powder, coffee, and salt.

2. In large bowl, with mixer at medium speed, beat butter and sugar until light and creamy. Reduce speed to low. Add vanilla; add eggs, one at a time, beating well after each addition. Beat in flour mixture until blended. With wooden spoon, stir in remaining 1 1/2 cups flour until blended. Divide dough in half. On ungreased large cookie sheet, with well-floured hands, shape dough into two 12" by 3" logs and place 3 inches apart. Bake logs until firm, 25 to 30 minutes. Cool on cookie sheet on wire rack 20 minutes.

3. Transfer logs to cutting board. With serrated knife, cut each log crosswise on diagonal into 1/2-inch-thick slices. Place slices, cut side down, on two ungreased large cookie sheets. Bake 20 minutes, turning slices once and rotating cookie sheets between upper and lower racks halfway through baking time. Transfer to racks to cool completely.

4. In heavy 1-quart saucepan, melt chocolate over low heat, stirring frequently, until smooth. With pastry brush, brush top of each biscotti with some melted chocolate; sprinkle some almonds on chocolate. Refrigerate biscotti until chocolate sets, about 30 minutes.

Each biscotti: About 110 calories, 2g protein, 13g carbohydrate, 6g total fat (3g saturated), 24mg cholesterol, 98mg sodium.

Chocolate Pretzels

Cooking with children became popular during this decade with special classes and cookbooks catering to junior chefs. Making these pretzel-shaped treats is a perfect project for kids and parents.

PREP: 1 HOUR PLUS COOLING   BAKE: 15 MINUTES PER BATCH
MAKES 36 PRETZELS

2 cups all-purpose flour
1/3 cup unsweetened cocoa
2 teaspoons baking powder
1/2 teaspoon salt
3/4 cup butter or margarine
   (11/2 sticks), softened

3/4 cup sugar
1 large egg
1 teaspoon vanilla extract
assorted sprinkles

1. Preheat oven to 350°F. In medium bowl, combine flour, cocoa, baking powder, and salt.

2. In large bowl, with mixer at medium speed, beat butter and sugar until creamy. Beat in egg and vanilla until well blended. At low speed, beat in flour mixture just until blended, occasionally scraping bowl with rubber spatula.

3. Divide dough in half. Wrap one piece of dough in plastic. Place sprinkles in pie plate.

4. Working with unwrapped portion of dough, on unfloured work surface, with hands shape tablespoons of dough into 9-inch-long ropes. Shape ropes into loop-shaped pretzels; press ends lightly to seal. Gently press pretzels, top side down, into sprinkles. Place pretzels, decorated side up, 1/2 inch apart, on ungreased large cookie sheet.

5. Bake pretzels until bottoms are lightly browned, about 15 minutes. With wide spatula, transfer pretzels to wire racks to cool completely.

6. Repeat with remaining piece of dough.

Each pretzel: About 80 calories, 1g protein, 10g carbohydrate, 4g total fat (3g saturated), 16mg cholesterol, 93mg sodium.

Florentines

Made with very little flour—but lots of almonds and candied orange peel—these elegant cookies are perfect for a reception or a special gift. Handle the cookies carefully when icing them, as they are quite fragile. For an even more lavish treat, sandwich two cookies together with a layer of chocolate in between.

PREP: 40 MINUTES   BAKE: 10 MINUTES PER BATCH
MAKES 48 COOKIES

6 tablespoons butter, cut into pieces (do not use margarine)	1 cup slivered almonds (4 ounces), finely chopped
1/4 cup heavy or whipping cream	1/2 cup candied orange peel, finely chopped
1 tablespoon light corn syrup	8 squares (8 ounces) semisweet chocolate, melted
1/2 cup sugar	
2 tablespoons all-purpose flour	

1. Preheat oven to 350°F. Line large cookie sheet with cooking parchment.
2. In 1-quart saucepan, combine butter, cream, corn syrup, sugar, and flour. Heat to boiling over medium heat, stirring frequently. Remove from heat; stir in almonds and candied orange peel.
3. Drop batter by rounded teaspoons, 3 inches apart, on prepared cookie sheet. Do not place more than 6 on cookie sheet. Bake just until set, about 10 minutes. Cool on cookie sheet on wire rack 1 minute. With wide spatula, transfer to racks to cool. If cookies become too hard to remove; return sheet to oven briefly to soften. Repeat with remaining batter.
4. With small metal spatula or butter knife, spread flat side of cookie with melted chocolate. Return to racks, chocolate side up; let stand until chocolate sets.

Each serving: About 70 calories, 1g protein, 8g carbohydrate, 5g total fat (2g saturated), 6mg cholesterol, 15mg sodium.

No-Bake Cookie Balls

In the 1950s there were many product-driven recipes, like these easy-to-make sugar-coated gems from the November 1953 issue of *Good Housekeeping*. Make them several days ahead so the flavors can fully develop.

PREP: 30 MINUTES   MAKES 48 COOKIES

2 teaspoons instant-coffee powder or granules

$1/3$ cup very hot water

6 squares (6 ounces) semisweet chocolate

1$1/3$ cups finely crushed vanilla-wafer cookies (about 36 cookies)

1 cup walnuts (4 ounces), toasted (page 97) and finely chopped

3 tablespoons light corn syrup

2 tablespoons dark rum or brandy (optional)

3 cups confectioners' sugar

1. In cup, dissolve instant coffee in hot water; set aside.

2. In 3-quart saucepan, melt chocolate over low heat, stirring frequently, until smooth. Remove from heat; with wooden spoon, stir in crushed cookies, walnuts, corn syrup, rum, if using, coffee, and 2$1/2$ cups confectioners' sugar until blended.

3. Roll dough into 1-inch balls. Roll balls in remaining $1/2$ cup confectioners' sugar until coated.

Each cookie: About 75 calories, 1g protein, 11g carbohydrate, 3g total fat (1g saturated), 0mg cholesterol, 15mg sodium.

Chocolate Icebox Cookies

Pair two of these thin rounds with your favorite frosting (or a thin layer of raspberry jam) to make some very classy sandwich cookies.

PREP: 25 MINUTES PLUS CHILLING   BAKE: 10 MINUTES PER BATCH
MAKES ABOUT 120 COOKIES

1²/₃ cups all-purpose flour
1/2 cup unsweetened cocoa
1 teaspoon baking powder
1/2 teaspoon baking soda
1/4 teaspoon salt
3/4 cup butter or margarine
    (1¹/₂ sticks), softened

1/2 cup granulated sugar
1/2 cup packed light brown sugar
2 squares (2 ounces) semisweet
    chocolate, melted and cooled
1 teaspoon vanilla extract
1 large egg

1. In medium bowl, combine flour, cocoa, baking powder, baking soda, and salt.

2. In large bowl, with mixer at medium speed, beat butter and granulated and brown sugars until light and fluffy. Beat in chocolate and vanilla until well combined. Beat in egg. Reduce speed to low; beat in flour mixture until blended.

3. Divide dough in half. On separate sheets of waxed paper, shape each piece of dough into 12" by 1½" log. Wrap each log in waxed paper and slide onto small cookie sheet for easier handling. Refrigerate dough until firm enough to slice, at least 2 hours, or up to overnight. (If using margarine, freeze overnight.)

4. Preheat oven to 350°F. Remove one dough log from refrigerator, keep remaining log refrigerated. Cut log into scant 1/4-inch-thick slices. Place slices, 1 inch apart, on two ungreased large cookie sheets. Bake 10 to 11 minutes, rotating cookie sheets between upper and lower racks halfway through baking. Cool on cookie sheets on wire racks 1 minute. With wide spatula, transfer cookies to racks to cool completely.

5. Repeat with remaining dough.

Each cookie: About 25 calories, 0g protein, 4g carbohydrate, 1g total fat (1g saturated), 5mg cholesterol, 25mg sodium.

Chocolate-Spice Refrigerator Crisps

We like to keep a brick of this dough in the freezer. It's great for impromptu visits. For the little ones, sandwich two together with a scoop of ice cream.

PREP: 30 MINUTES PLUS CHILLING AND COOLING
BAKE: 12 MINUTES PER BATCH
MAKES 78 COOKIES

1 3/4 cups all-purpose flour
1/2 cup unsweetened cocoa
1 1/2 teaspoons cinnamon
1 teaspoon baking powder
1/2 teaspoon baking soda
1/2 teaspoon ground ginger
1/4 teaspoon ground nutmeg
1/4 teaspoon salt
1/4 teaspoon finely ground
   black pepper

3/4 cup butter or margarine
   (1 1/2 sticks), softened
1/2 cup plus 1/3 cup granulated sugar
1/2 cup packed light brown sugar
2 squares (2 ounces) semisweet
   chocolate, melted and cooled
1 large egg
1 teaspoon vanilla extract

1. In medium bowl, combine flour, cocoa, cinnamon, baking powder, baking soda, ginger, nutmeg, salt, and pepper.
2. In large bowl, with mixer at medium speed, beat butter, 1/2 cup granulated sugar, and brown sugar until creamy, occasionally scraping bowl with rubber spatula. Beat in chocolate, egg, and vanilla, until combined. Reduce speed to low. Gradually add flour mixture; beat until blended, occasionally scraping bowl.
3. Divide dough in half. On waxed paper, shape one piece of dough into 10" by 12" by 1" brick. Wrap brick in plastic wrap and slide onto small cookie sheet for easier handling. Repeat with remaining piece of dough. Refrigerate dough bricks until firm enough to slice, at least 2 hours or up to overnight. (Or, place dough in freezer 30 minutes.)
4. Preheat oven to 350°F. Place remaining 1/3 cup granulated sugar on small plate. Place 1 dough brick on cutting board (keep remaining brick in refrigerator). Cut crosswise into scant 1/4-inch-thick slices. Coat each

slice, on both sides, in granulated sugar. Place coated slices, 1 inch apart, on two ungreased large cookie sheets. Bake 12 minutes, rotating cookies sheets between upper and lower racks halfway through baking. Cool on cookie sheets on wire racks 1 minute. With wide spatula, transfer cookies to racks to cool completely.

5. Repeat with remaining dough and sugar.

Each cookie: About 45 calories, 1g protein, 6g carbohydrate, 2g total fat (1g saturated), 8mg cholesterol, 40mg sodium.

CONFECTIONS

Chocolate Truffles

To add extra flavor to these easy-to-make bittersweet confections, stir two tablespoons of a favorite liqueur, such as Grand Marnier, or brandy into the melted chocolate mixture.

PREP: 25 MINUTES PLUS CHILLING   MAKES 32 TRUFFLES

8 ounces bittersweet chocolate or
  6 squares (6 ounces) semisweet
  chocolate plus 2 squares
  (2 ounces) unsweetened chocolate
1/2 cup heavy or whipping cream
3 tablespoons unsalted butter,
  cut into pieces and softened
  (do not use margarine)

1/3 cup hazelnuts (filberts), toasted
  and skinned (page 97), and finely
  chopped
3 tablespoons unsweetened cocoa

1. Line 9" by 5" metal loaf pan with plastic wrap. In food processor with knife blade attached, process chocolate until finely ground.

2. In 1-quart saucepan, heat cream to boiling over medium-high heat. Add cream to chocolate in food processor; process until smooth. Add butter; process to blend well.

3. Pour chocolate mixture into prepared pan; spread evenly. Refrigerate until cool and firm enough to handle, about 3 hours.

4. Place hazelnuts in small bowl, place cocoa in another small bowl. Remove chocolate mixture from pan by lifting edges of plastic wrap; invert chocolate block onto cutting board. Discard plastic. Cut chocolate block into 32 pieces. (To cut chocolate mixture easily, dip knife in hot water and wipe dry.) With cool hands, quickly roll each piece into a ball. One at a time, roll half of balls in hazelnuts and roll remaining balls in cocoa. Place in single layer in waxed paper–lined airtight container. Refrigerate up to 1 week or freeze up to 1 month. Remove from freezer 5 minutes before serving.

Each truffle: About 65 calories, 1g protein, 5g carbohydrate, 6g total fat (3g saturated), 8mg cholesterol, 2mg sodium.

Amaretto Truffles

This recipe is so easy to prepare, you'll be able to make many batches to give all your friends and family for the holiday. Place each truffle in a fluted foil or paper cup.

PREP: 25 MINUTES PLUS CHILLING   MAKES 64 TRUFFLES

10 squares (10 ounces) semisweet
   chocolate
2 squares (2 ounces) unsweetened
   chocolate
3/4 cup heavy or whipping cream
5 tablespoons unsalted butter,
   cut into pieces and softened
   (do not use margarine)

1/4 cup almond-flavored liqueur
1/3 cup blanched almonds, toasted
   (page 97) and finely chopped
1/4 cup unsweetened cocoa

1. Grease 8-inch square baking pan; line with plastic wrap. In food processor with knife blade attached, process semisweet and unsweetened chocolates until very finely ground.

2. In 1-quart saucepan, heat cream to boiling over medium-high heat. With food processor running, add hot cream, butter, and liqueur to chocolate; blend until smooth.

3. Pour chocolate mixture into pan; spread evenly. Refrigerate chocolate mixture until cool and firm enough to handle, at least 3 hours, or freeze 1 hour.

4. Place chopped almonds in small bowl; place cocoa in another small bowl. Invert chocolate block onto cutting board; discard plastic wrap. Cut chocolate block into 8 strips, then cut each strip crosswise into 8 squares. (To cut chocolate block neatly, dip knife in hot water and wipe dry.)

5. One at a time, roll half of chocolate squares in chopped almonds and remaining squares in cocoa. Place truffles in single layer in waxed paper–lined airtight container. Refrigerate up to 2 weeks or freeze up to 1 month. Remove from freezer 5 minutes before serving.

Each truffle: About 55 calories, 1g protein, 4g carbohydrate, 4g total fat (2g saturated), 6mg cholesterol, 1mg sodium.

Mocha Truffles

Make these truffles up to two weeks ahead—they're perfect for holiday gift-giving.

PREP: 30 MINUTES PLUS CHILLING   MAKES 48 TRUFFLES

12 squares (12 ounces) semisweet
   chocolate, coarsely chopped
3/4 cup sweetened condensed milk
1 tablespoon instant-coffee powder
   or granules

2 tablespoons coffee-flavored liqueur
1/8 teaspoon salt
1/2 cup unsweetened cocoa

1. In heavy 2-quart saucepan, melt chocolate over low heat, stirring frequently, until smooth. Stir in sweetened condensed milk, coffee powder, liqueur, and salt until well mixed. Refrigerate mixture until easy to shape, about 30 minutes.

2. Place cocoa in small bowl. Dust hands with cocoa, then shape 1 rounded teaspoon chocolate mixture into a ball. Dip ball in cocoa to coat. Repeat with remaining chocolate mixture. Place truffles in single layer in waxed paper–lined airtight container. Refrigerate up to 2 weeks or freeze up to 1 month. Remove from freezer 5 minutes before serving.

Each truffle: About 55 calories, 1g protein, 7g carbohydrate, 3g total fat (2g saturated), 2mg cholesterol, 10mg sodium.

Crackly Chocolate Almonds

Toasting almonds accomplishes two things: it crisps them up and brings out their flavor.

PREP: 1 HOUR 10 MINUTES PLUS COOLING   BAKE: 15 MINUTES
MAKES 8 CUPS

4 cups whole blanched almonds (1 pound)	1 teaspoon vanilla extract
1¼ cups sugar	1 pound bittersweet or semisweet chocolate, chopped
¼ cup water	⅓ cup unsweetened cocoa

1. Preheat oven to 350°F. Spread almonds in two jelly-roll pans or on two cookie sheets. Bake, stirring occasionally, until toasted, 15 minutes. Cool.

2. Line same jelly-roll pans with parchment or foil. In heavy 4-quart saucepan, combine almonds, sugar, water, and vanilla. Cook, stirring constantly, over medium-high heat until sugar becomes thick and cloudy and crystallizes on side of saucepan and almonds are coated and separate, 5 to 6 minutes. With slotted spoon, transfer almonds to jelly-roll pans, leaving any excess sugar in saucepan. Spread almonds out; refrigerate until cold, about 45 minutes.

3. Meanwhile, in large microwave-safe bowl, melt half of chocolate in microwave oven on High for 1½ to 2 minutes; stir until smooth. Cool slightly.

4. With hands, transfer almonds from one pan to chocolate in bowl; discard any excess sugar in pan. With wooden spoon, stir until almonds are completely coated with chocolate. Line same jelly-roll pan with parchment paper; spoon almonds into pan. With fork, spread out almonds and separate as much as possible. Repeat with remaining chocolate and almonds. Refrigerate until chocolate is set, about 1 hour.

5. Sift cocoa into large bowl. Break almonds apart to create single almonds. Add almonds, in batches, to cocoa, tossing to coat well. (If you want some variations in color, toss about three-fourths of the almonds in cocoa and leave the remaining nuts uncoated.) Place cocoa-coated almonds in sieve and gently shake to remove excess cocoa. Place almonds in airtight container. Refrigerate up to 1 month.

Each ¼ cup: About 175 calories, 4g protein, 16g carbohydrate, 12g total fat (3g saturated), 0mg cholesterol, 2mg sodium.

Peanut-Chocolate Balls

Finely chopped peanuts add a crunchy coating to these rich candies.

PREP: 45 MINUTES PLUS CHILLING   COOK: 5 MINUTES
MAKES 72 CANDIES

1 cup creamy peanut butter
1 cup confectioners' sugar
1 tablespoon honey
6 squares (6 ounces) semisweet
  chocolate, coarsely chopped

1 tablespoon vegetable shortening
2 cups dry-roasted peanuts, finely
  chopped

1. Line jelly-roll pan with waxed paper. In medium bowl stir peanut butter, confectioners' sugar, and honey until well blended, kneading with hands if necessary.

2. Shape peanut butter mixture into 3/4-inch balls; place in jelly-roll pan. Cover and refrigerate until firm, about 2 hours.

3. When peanut butter balls are firm, in 1-quart saucepan, melt chocolate and shortening over low heat, stirring frequently, until smooth. Remove from heat; cool slightly.

4. Place chopped peanuts in small bowl. With fork, carefully dip peanut butter balls into chocolate mixture. Then, using fork, roll balls in peanuts to coat. Return coated balls to jelly-roll pan. Loosely cover pan; refrigerate until coating sets, about 1 hour. Layer between waxed paper in airtight container. Refrigerate up to 2 weeks.

Each candy: About 65 calories, 2g protein, 5g carbohydrate, 5g total fat (1g saturated), 0mg cholesterol, 50mg sodium.

Chocolate Panforte

This rich, dense confection is a specialty of Siena, Italy. It's delicious with an espresso or as an accompaniment to cheese.

PREP: 30 MINUTES PLUS COOLING AND STANDING OVERNIGHT
BAKE: 20 MINUTES   MAKES 24 SERVINGS

1/4 cup all-purpose flour

1/4 cup unsweetened cocoa

3 ounces bittersweet chocolate, grated, or 1/2 cup semisweet chocolate chips

1/2 teaspoon ground cinnamon

1/8 teaspoon ground cloves

1/8 teaspoon ground ginger

1/8 teaspoon ground nutmeg

3/4 cup chopped candied orange peel

1 tablespoon grated fresh orange peel

1 cup blanched almonds (4 ounces), toasted and coarsely chopped

1 cup hazelnuts (4 ounces), toasted, skinned (page 97), and coarsely chopped

3/4 cup packed light brown sugar

1/3 cup honey

2 tablespoons unsalted butter or margarine

1 tablespoon water

confectioners' sugar

1. Preheat oven to 325°F. Line 9-inch pie pan or 8-inch round cake pan with foil, extending foil over rim of pan. Lightly oil foil.

2. In large bowl, combine flour, cocoa, chocolate, cinnamon, cloves, ginger, nutmeg, candied orange peel, fresh orange peel, almonds, and hazelnuts.

3. In heavy 2-quart saucepan, combine brown sugar, honey, butter, and water; stir until blended. Heat to rolling boil over medium heat. Boil, stirring constantly, 1 minute. Remove from heat; immediately pour hot sugar mixture over chocolate-nut mixture, stirring to coat nuts. Pour into prepared pan; spread to form smooth, even layer.

4. Bake until panforte starts to bubble around edge, about 20 minutes. Place panforte in pan on wire rack. Cool completely.

5. When cool, remove panforte from pan by lifting edges of foil; peel away foil. Invert onto rack, so bottom is facing up. Wrap panforte in foil. Store in airtight container at room temperature up to 1 week or refrigerate up to 3 weeks. (Allow panforte to age for at least 1 day before serving.)

6. To serve, unwrap panforte. Place stencil with small star cutouts on top. Sprinkle confectioners' sugar through fine-mesh sieve over stencil. Carefully lift off stencil. Slice panforte into thin wedges.

Each serving: About 155 calories, 3g protein, 20g carbohydrate, 8g total fat (2g saturated), 3mg cholesterol, 5mg sodium.

Peanut Butter Cups

Just enough for two bites—a luscious homemade version of everyone's favorite candy.

PREP: 40 MINUTES PLUS CHILLING   MAKES 60 CANDIES

9 ounces white chocolate, Swiss confectionery bars, or white baking bars, chopped

1¹/₂ cups creamy peanut butter

8 squares (8 ounces) semisweet chocolate, chopped

¹/₃ cup lightly salted peanuts, chopped

1. Arrange 60 miniature (1" by ¹/₄") paper or foil baking cups in jelly-roll pan.

2. In heavy 2-quart saucepan, heat white chocolate and ³/₄ cup peanut butter over low heat, stirring occasionally, until melted and smooth. Divide peanut butter mixture evenly among baking cups. Refrigerate 10 minutes.

3. Meanwhile, in heavy 2-quart saucepan, heat semisweet chocolate and remaining ³/₄ cup peanut butter over low heat, stirring occasionally, until melted and smooth.

4. Spoon warm chocolate–peanut butter mixture on top of chilled mixture in baking cups; sprinkle with peanuts. Refrigerate overnight. Store candies in airtight container in single layer. Refrigerate for up to 1 week or freeze up to 1 month.

Each candy: About 85 calories, 2g protein, 7g carbohydrate, 6g total fat (2g saturated), 1mg cholesterol, 40mg sodium.

Creamy Fudge

A silky smooth candy treat you can make up to one month ahead and freeze.

PREP: 10 MINUTES PLUS CHILLING   COOK: 5 MINUTES
MAKES 64 PIECES

16 squares (16 ounces) semisweet
   chocolate, chopped
1 square (1 ounce) unsweetened
   chocolate, chopped
1 can (14 ounces) sweetened

condensed milk
1 1/2 teaspoons vanilla extract
1/8 teaspoon salt

1. Line 8-inch square baking pan with foil, extending foil above rim of opposite sides.
2. In 2-quart saucepan, combine semisweet and unsweetened chocolates and condensed milk. Cook, stirring constantly, over medium–low heat until chocolates have melted and mixture is smooth, about 5 minutes.
3. Remove saucepan from heat; stir in vanilla and salt. Pour chocolate mixture into prepared pan; spread evenly. Refrigerate until firm, at least 4 hours or up to overnight.
4. Remove fudge from pan by lifting edges of foil. Invert fudge onto cutting board; discard foil. Cut into 8 strips, then cut each strip crosswise into 8 pieces. Place pieces between waxed paper in airtight container. Store at room temperature up to 1 week, or refrigerate up to 1 month.

Each piece: About 55 calories, 1g protein, 8g carbohydrate, 3g total fat (2g saturated), 2mg cholesterol, 15mg sodium.

Chocolate-Walnut Fudge

Prepare as directed but stir in **1 cup walnuts (4 ounces),** coarsely chopped with vanilla and salt.

Each piece: About 67 calories, 1g protein, 8g carbohydrate, 4g total fat (2g saturated), 2mg cholesterol, 13mg sodium.

Chunky Black and White Chocolate Bark

Filled with dried cranberries and pistachio nuts, our version of chocolate bark is the perfect holiday treat. Pack it into small boxes or cellophane bags and tie them up with red and green ribbons.

PREP: 20 MINUTES PLUS CHILLING   MAKES 1 3/4 POUNDS

1 cup shelled pistachios
  (about 8 ounces unshelled)
12 squares (12 ounces) semisweet
  chocolate, chopped

8 ounces white chocolate, Swiss
  confectionery bars, or white baking
  bars, chopped
3/4 cup dried cranberries

1. Preheat oven to 350°F. Place pistachios in medium baking pan; toast in oven, stirring occasionally, until lightly browned, 10 to 15 minutes. Cool in pan on wire rack.

2. Meanwhile in 2-quart saucepan, melt semisweet chocolate over low heat, stirring frequently, until smooth. In 1-quart saucepan, melt white chocolate over low heat, stirring frequently, until smooth. Remove pans from heat.

3. In small bowl, combine pistachios and cranberries. Stir half of nut mixture into semisweet chocolate. On large cookie sheet, with small metal spatula, spread semisweet-chocolate mixture to about 1/4-inch thickness. Drop white chocolate by tablespoons on top of semisweet chocolate mixture. With tip of knife, swirl chocolates together for marbled effect. Sprinkle with remaining nut mixture. Refrigerate until firm, about 1 hour. Break bark into pieces. Layer between waxed paper in airtight container. Refrigerate up to 1 month.

Each ounce: About 140 calories, 2g protein, 16g carbohydrate, 9g total fat (4g saturated), 1mg cholesterol, 10mg sodium.

Chocolate-Dipped Dried Fruit

This recipe can be doubled to make enough to serve a crowd. After several tries we found that it is easiest if the larger pieces of fruit are dipped first. We used dried apricots, apples, pears, and pineapple, but you can use other fruits, such as peaches and mango.

PREP: 10 MINUTES PLUS COOLING   COOK: 5 MINUTES
MAKES ABOUT 33 PIECES DIPPED FRUIT

4 squares (4 ounces) semisweet
  chocolate, chopped
1 teaspoon vegetable shortening

1 pound mixed dried fruit, such as
  apricots, apples, pears, and
  pineapple
3 ounces crystallized ginger (optional)

1. Place sheet of waxed paper under large wire rack. In top of double boiler or in small metal bowl set over 2-quart saucepan (double-boiler top or bowl should be 2 inches above water), melt chocolate and shortening, stirring frequently, until smooth.

2. With fingers, dip one piece of fruit at a time halfway into chocolate. Shake off excess chocolate or gently scrape fruit across rim of double boiler, being careful not to remove too much chocolate. Place dipped fruit on wire rack; set aside until chocolate is set, at least 1 hour.

3. Layer fruit between waxed paper in airtight container. Store at room temperature up to 1 week.

Each piece: About 55 calories, 1g protein, 12g carbohydrate, 1g total fat (1g saturated), 0mg cholesterol, 2mg sodium.

DESSERTS

This may well become your favorite chapter. It is filled with silky puddings, light-as-a-feather soufflés, and the most luscious ice-cream desserts ever.

Custards and Puddings

Custard is a mixture of milk (or cream) that is sweetened with sugar and thickened with eggs. When making custard, the eggs should be gently stirred into the milk mixture to create as few bubbles as possible. Custards need moderate cooking temperature, so they are always baked in a water bath: a roasting pan filled with enough hot water to come halfway up the side of the custard. For stirred custards, the yolks must be gradually heated to avoid curdling. To do this, a small amount of the hot milk is first stirred into the egg yolks to warm them, a technique called tempering.

Sauce Smarts

A custard sauce needs special care. To prevent overcooking or curdling, it is constantly stirred over low heat until the sauce can coat the back of a spoon (if you draw a finger through the sauce, it will leave a path). The doneness can also be checked with an instant-read thermometer. The temperature should range between 160° and 170°F.

Soufflé Savvy

The secret to a high-rising soufflé is perfectly beaten egg whites. Room-temperature egg whites beat to their highest volume, but eggs separate most easily when cold. Once separated, let them stand at room temperature for about 30 minutes to warm them. Beat egg whites just until stiff—not dry. Overbeaten whites look cottony and clumpy.

Meringue Magic

Here are some tips for whipping up a perfect meringue:
- Don't make meringue on a humid day.
- Make sure the bowl and beaters do not have any fat on them.
- Beat the egg whites until soft peaks form, then gradually add the sugar, beating until stiff peaks form.
- Rub a bit of meringue between your fingers to be sure the sugar has dissolved.

Chocolate Fondue with Fruit

Dipping succulent chunks of fresh fruit into a rich chocolate sauce is a delicious way to end a meal with friends. We suggest using bananas, pears, and strawberries, but almost any in-season fruit will do. During the summer, use apricots, peaches, or nectarines, and in the fall choose a variety of apples: sweet, tart, and something in between.

PREP: 15 MINUTES   COOK 5 MINUTES   MAKES 8 SERVINGS

6 squares (6 ounces) semisweet chocolate, coarsely chopped

1/2 cup half-and-half or light cream

1/2 teaspoon vanilla extract

4 small bananas, peeled and cut into 1/2-inch-thick slices

2 to 3 small pears, cored and cut into 1/2-inch-thick wedges

1 pint strawberries, hulled

1/2 cup finely chopped almonds, toasted (page 97)

1. In 1-quart saucepan, heat chocolate and half-and-half over low heat, stirring frequently, until chocolate has melted and mixture is smooth, about 5 minutes. Stir in vanilla; keep warm.

2. To serve, arrange bananas, pears, and strawberries on large platter. Spoon sauce into small bowl; place nuts in separate small bowl. With forks or toothpicks, have guests dip fruit into chocolate sauce, then into nuts.

Each serving: About 249 calories, 4g protein, 36g carbohydrate, 13g total fat (5g saturated), 6mg cholesterol, 10mg sodium.

Chocolate Soufflés

Soufflés always make an impressive dessert. They are irresistible as individual soufflés and spectacular when baked as one large soufflé.

PREP: 20 MINUTES PLUS COOLING   BAKE: 25 MINUTES
MAKES 8 SERVINGS

1¼ cups plus 3 tablespoons granulated sugar
2 tablespoons cornstarch
1 teaspoon instant espresso-coffee powder
1 cup milk
5 squares (5 ounces) unsweetened chocolate, chopped

3 tablespoons butter or margarine, softened
4 large eggs, separated
2 teaspoons vanilla extract
2 large egg whites
¼ teaspoon salt
confectioners' sugar

1. In 3-quart saucepan, combine 1¼ cups granulated sugar, cornstarch, and espresso powder. With wire whisk, gradually stir in milk until blended. Cook over medium heat, stirring constantly, until mixture has thickened and boils; boil, stirring, 1 minute. Remove from heat.

2. Stir in chocolate and butter until melted and smooth. With whisk, beat in egg yolks until well blended; stir in vanilla. Cool to lukewarm, stirring constantly.

3. Meanwhile, preheat oven to 350°F. Grease eight 6-ounce custard cups or ramekins; sprinkle lightly with remaining 3 tablespoons granulated sugar.

4. In large bowl, with mixer at high speed, beat 6 egg whites and salt just until stiff peaks form when beaters are lifted. Gently fold one-third of beaten egg whites into chocolate mixture; fold back into remaining egg whites just until blended.

5. Spoon into prepared custard cups. Place in jelly-roll pan for easier handling. Bake until soufflés have puffed and centers are glossy, 25 to 30 minutes. Dust with confectioners' sugar. Serve immediately.

Each serving: About 356 calories, 7g protein, 44g carbohydrate, 19g total fat (10g saturated), 122mg cholesterol, 178mg sodium.

Amaretto-Chocolate Soufflé

This irresistibly rich dessert is the kind of sublime treat you'd expect to find on the menu at an upscale restaurant—and you don't have to make a reservation to enjoy it!

PREP: 20 MINUTES   BAKE: 40 MINUTES
MAKES: 10 SERVINGS

1/4 cup all-purpose flour
1 cup plus 2 tablespoons granulated
  sugar
1 teaspoon instant espresso-coffee
  powder
1 cup milk
5 squares (5 ounces) unsweetened
  chocolate, coarsely chopped

3 tablespoons butter or margarine
4 large eggs, separated
3 tablespoons almond-flavored liqueur
2 teaspoons vanilla extract
2 large egg whites
1/4 teaspoon salt
confectioners' sugar

1. In 3-quart saucepan, combine flour, 1/2 cup granulated sugar, and espresso powder. With wire whisk, gradually stir in milk until blended. Cook over medium heat, stirring constantly, until mixture has thickened and boils; boil, stirring, 1 minute. Remove from heat.

2. Stir in chocolate and butter. With whisk, beat in egg yolks until well blended; stir in liqueur and vanilla. Cool to lukewarm, stirring occasionally.

3. Meanwhile, preheat oven to 350°F. Grease 2-quart soufflé dish; sprinkle with 2 tablespoons granulated sugar.

4. In large bowl, with mixer at high speed, beat 6 egg whites and salt until foamy. Sprinkle in remaining 1/2 cup granulated sugar, 2 tablespoons at a time, beating until sugar has dissolved and egg whites stand in stiff, glossy peaks when beaters are lifted. Gently fold two-thirds of beaten egg whites, one-third at a time, into chocolate mixture, just until blended. Fold chocolate mixture back into remaining whites, just until blended.

5. Pour chocolate mixture into prepared soufflé dish. Bake until soufflé has puffed, about 40 minutes. Dust with confectioners' sugar. Serve immediately.

Each serving: About 270 calories, 6g protein, 33g carbohydrate, 14g total fat (8g saturated), 97mg cholesterol, 144mg sodium.

Brownie Pudding Cake

Two desserts for the price of one! It separates during baking into a fudgy brownie on top of a silky chocolate pudding.

PREP: 20 MINUTES   BAKE: 30 MINUTES
MAKES 8 SERVINGS

2 teaspoons instant-coffee powder
  (optional)
2 tablespoons (optional) plus
  1³/₄ cups boiling water
1 cup all-purpose flour
³/₄ cup unsweetened cocoa
¹/₂ cup granulated sugar
2 teaspoons baking powder
¹/₄ teaspoon salt

¹/₂ cup milk
4 tablespoons butter or margarine,
  melted
1 teaspoon vanilla extract
¹/₂ cup packed brown sugar
whipped cream or vanilla ice cream
  (optional)

1. Preheat oven to 350°F. In cup, dissolve coffee powder in 2 tablespoons boiling water, if using.

2. In large bowl, combine flour, ¹/₂ cup cocoa, granulated sugar, baking powder, and salt. In measuring cup, combine milk, melted butter, vanilla, and coffee, if using. With wooden spoon, stir milk mixture into flour mixture until just blended. Pour into ungreased 8-inch square baking dish.

3. In small bowl, thoroughly combine brown sugar and remaining ¹/₄ cup cocoa; sprinkle evenly over batter. Carefully pour remaining 1³/₄ cups boiling water evenly over mixture in baking dish; do not stir.

4. Bake 30 minutes (batter will separate into cake and pudding layers). Cool in pan on wire rack 10 minutes. Serve hot with whipped cream or ice cream, if you like.

Each serving: About 238 calories, 4g protein, 43g carbohydrate, 7g total fat (5g saturated), 18mg cholesterol, 267mg sodium.

Quick Chocolate Pudding Cake

Pudding cake is easy to prepare, especially when the recipe includes buttermilk baking mix, as does ours. This dessert is best eaten warm and is especially fabulous topped with a dollop of whipped cream. If you like, use a vegetable peeler to shave chocolate over the cream.

PREP: 10 MINUTES   BAKE: 30 MINUTES
MAKES 6 SERVINGS

1 cup all-purpose buttermilk
   baking mix
3/4 unsweetened cocoa
1/3 cup granulated sugar
1/4 cup packed brown sugar

4 tablespoons butter or margarine
1/2 cup milk
1 teaspoon vanilla extract
1 3/4 cups boiling water
whipped cream (optional)

1. Preheat oven to 350°F. In medium bowl, combine baking mix, 1/2 cup cocoa, and granulated sugar. In small bowl, combine brown sugar and remaining 1/4 cup cocoa.

2. In small microwave-safe bowl, heat butter in microwave oven on High 45 seconds, or just until butter melts, stirring once. Stir butter, milk, and vanilla into baking mix mixture until blended. Pour batter into ungreased 8-inch square baking dish. Sprinkle evenly with brown-sugar mixture. Pour boiling water evenly over mixture in baking dish. Bake 30 minutes (batter will separate into cake and pudding layers). Cool in pan on wire rack 5 minutes. Serve warm with whipped cream, if you like.

Each serving: About 265 calories, 4g protein, 39g carbohydrate, 13g total fat (7g saturated), 23mg cholesterol, 360mg sodium.

Chocolate Bread Pudding

For this pudding, cubes of bread are steeped in chocolate custard and then layered with ribbons of melted semisweet chocolate.

PREP: 25 MINUTES PLUS CHILLING   BAKE: 50 MINUTES
MAKES 8 SERVINGS

8 slices stale firm white bread,
  cut into 1-inch pieces
3 tablespoons plus 1/3 cup sugar
8 squares (8 ounces) semisweet
  chocolate, melted

3 cups milk
3 large eggs
1 1/2 teaspoons vanilla extract

1. Grease 8-inch square baking dish. Scatter one-third of bread pieces in prepared dish in even layer; sprinkle with 1 tablespoon sugar and drizzle with 2 tablespoons melted chocolate. Repeat layers. Top with remaining bread pieces.
2. In 2-quart saucepan, heat milk to simmering over medium-high heat.
3. Meanwhile, in medium bowl, with wire whisk, combine eggs and 1/3 cup sugar. While whisking constantly, slowly pour simmering milk into egg mixture. Stir in remaining melted chocolate and vanilla.
4. Pour egg mixture over bread. Refrigerate until bread has absorbed chocolate mixture, gently stirring mixture occasionally, about 3 hours.
5. Meanwhile, preheat oven to 325°F. Sprinkle pudding with remaining 1 tablespoon sugar. Place dish in medium roasting pan; place in oven. Carefully pour enough boiling water into roasting pan to come halfway up sides of dish. Bake until knife inserted in center of pudding comes out clean, about 50 minutes. Remove dish from roasting pan. Place on wire rack to cool 15 minutes. Serve pudding warm, or cover and refrigerate to serve cold later.

Each serving: About 355 calories, 9g protein, 49g carbohydrate, 15g total fat (8g saturated), 93mg cholesterol, 225mg sodium.

Chocolate-Cherry Bread Pudding

Perfect for chocoholics in search of some good old-fashioned comfort food. This pudding is delicious as is, but it is even better when served with by softly whipped cream flavored with a splash of kirsch or vanilla.

PREP: 20 MINUTES PLUS STANDING AND CHILLING   BAKE: 55 MINUTES
MAKES 8 SERVINGS

3 1/2 cups milk
4 squares (4 ounces) semisweet
  chocolate
2 squares (2 ounces) unsweetened
  chocolate
1/2 cup sugar
2 teaspoons vanilla extract

1/2 teaspoon salt
3 large eggs
8 ounces (about 10 slices) stale
  firm white bread, cut into
  1/4-inch pieces
1/2 cup dried tart cherries

1. Grease 8-inch square baking dish. In 2-quart saucepan, heat milk to simmering over medium-high heat.

2. Meanwhile, in 3-quart saucepan, melt semisweet and unsweetened chocolates over low heat, stirring frequently, until smooth. Remove from heat. With wire whisk, stir in sugar, vanilla, and salt. Stir in eggs, until combined. Slowly whisk simmering milk into melted-chocolate mixture until blended. Gently stir in bread. Let stand 20 minutes to allow bread to absorb milk mixture, stirring once.

3. Meanwhile, preheat oven to 325°F. Pour bread mixture into prepared baking dish; sprinkle with cherries. Cover with foil; bake 40 minutes. Uncover and bake until knife inserted in center of pudding comes out almost clean, about 15 minutes longer. Cool in pan on wire rack 20 minutes to serve warm, or cover and refrigerate to serve cold later.

Each serving: About 350 calories, 10g protein, 48g carbohydrate, 15g total fat (8g saturated), 95mg cholesterol, 375mg sodium.

Chocolate Pudding

Retro food at its best—and who doesn't love chocolate pudding? The good news is this treat has only 2 grams of fat per serving and tastes divine warm or chilled.

PREP: 5 MINUTES   COOK: 6 MINUTES
MAKES 4 SERVINGS

¹/₃ cup sugar	2 cups fat-free milk
¹/₄ cup cornstarch	1 square (1 ounce) semisweet
3 tablespoons unsweetened cocoa	chocolate, finely chopped
pinch salt	1 teaspoon vanilla extract

1. In 2-quart saucepan, with wire whisk, mix sugar, cornstarch, cocoa, and salt until combined. Whisk in milk until blended. Heat mixture to boiling over medium heat, stirring constantly. Add chocolate; cook 1 minute, stirring, until chocolate has melted and pudding thickens slightly. Remove from heat; stir in vanilla.

2. Spoon pudding into custard cups. Serve warm or place plastic wrap directly on surface of pudding and refrigerate to serve cold later.

Each serving: About 180 calories, 5g protein, 37g carbohydrate, 2g total fat (0g saturated), 2mg cholesterol, 105mg sodium.

Chocolate Pôts De Crème

These rich chocolate custards are the perfect ending to an elegant dinner. They can be prepared at least several hours ahead or even the day before. For a fancy presentation, top each serving with a whipped cream rosette and a candied coffee bean, candied rose or violet, or fat chocolate curl.

PREP: 15 MINUTES PLUS CHILLING AND COOLING   BAKE: 30 MINUTES
MAKES 6 SERVINGS

3 squares (3 ounces) semisweet
  chocolate, chopped
2¹/₂ cups milk
2 large eggs

2 large egg yolks
¹/₄ cup sugar
1 teaspoon vanilla extract

1. Preheat oven to 350°F. In 3-quart saucepan, heat chocolate and ¹/₄ cup milk over low heat, stirring frequently, until chocolate has melted and mixture is smooth; remove from heat.

2. In 2-quart saucepan, heat remaining 2¹/₄ cups milk to boiling over medium-high heat; stir into chocolate mixture until blended. In large bowl, whisk eggs, egg yolks, sugar, and vanilla until well blended. Gradually whisk in chocolate mixture until well combined. Pour into six 6-ounce ramekins or custard cups.

3. Place ramekins in medium roasting pan; place in oven. Carefully pour enough boiling water into roasting pan to come halfway up sides of ramekins. Cover roasting pan with foil, crimping edges loosely. Bake custards until knife inserted halfway between edge and center of custard comes out clean, 30 to 35 minutes. Remove foil; transfer ramekins to wire rack to cool. Refrigerate until well chilled, about 3 hours.

Each serving: About 210 calories, 7g protein, 22g carbohydrate, 11g total fat (6g saturated), 156mg cholesterol, 75mg sodium.

Baked Chocolate-Hazelnut Puddings

Bake this rich soufflélike dessert in individual ramekins. If you like, substitute toasted blanched almonds for the hazelnuts.

PREP: 30 MINUTES PLUS CHILLING   BAKE: 25 MINUTES
MAKES: 8 SERVINGS

3/4 cup hazelnuts (filberts), toasted
  and skinned (page 97)
3/4 cup sugar
4 tablespoons butter or margarine,
  softened
7 large eggs, separated

8 squares (8 ounces) semisweet
  chocolate, melted and cooled
1/4 teaspoon salt
3/4 cup heavy or whipping cream
1 teaspoon vanilla extract

1. Generously butter eight 6-ounce ramekins.
2. In food processor with knife blade attached, pulse hazelnuts with 1/4 cup sugar until finely ground.
3. In large bowl, with mixer at medium speed, beat butter until smooth. Add 1/4 cup sugar; beat until creamy. Add egg yolks, one at a time, beating well after each addition. Beat in nut mixture and chocolate until blended.
4. In another large bowl, with mixer at high speed, beat egg whites and salt until soft peaks form when beaters are lifted. Sprinkle in remaining 1/4 cup sugar, 2 tablespoons at a time, beating until sugar has dissolved and egg whites stand in stiff, glossy peaks when beaters are lifted. Stir one-fourth of beaten whites into chocolate mixture until well combined. Gently fold remaining whites into chocolate mixture just until blended. Spoon batter into prepared ramekins. Cover and refrigerate 4 hours or up to overnight.
5. Meanwhile, preheat oven to 350°F. Place ramekins in large roasting pan; place pan in oven. Pour enough boiling water into roasting pan to come halfway up sides of ramekins. Bake until knife blade inserted in center comes out with some fudgy batter clinging, about 25 minutes. Transfer ramekins to wire rack to cool 5 minutes.

6. Meanwhile, in small bowl, with mixer at medium speed, beat cream and vanilla until soft peaks form.

7. To serve, scoop out small amount of pudding from top of each dessert; fill with some whipped cream. Replace scooped-out pudding.

Each serving: About 500 calories, 10g protein, 37g carbohydrate, 37g total fat (17g saturated), 235mg cholesterol, 215mg sodium.

Chocolate Sticky Toffee Pudding

This classic British sweet is enjoying a resurgence in popularity. We devised a chocolate version of this moist, puddinglike cake—and didn't skimp on the heavenly caramel topping.

PREP: 30 MINUTES PLUS STANDING AND COOLING   BAKE: 18 MINUTES
MAKES 12 SERVINGS

3/4 cup water
1/2 cup chopped pitted dates
1 teaspoon instant-coffee powder or granules
1/2 teaspoon baking soda
1/2 cup all-purpose flour
1/3 cup unsweetened cocoa
1/2 teaspoon baking powder
1/4 teaspoon salt

5 tablespoons butter or margarine, softened
1/2 cup granulated sugar
1 large egg
1/2 teaspoon vanilla extract
1/2 cup packed light brown sugar
2 tablespoons heavy or whipping cream
whipped cream (optional)

1. Preheat oven to 350°F. Grease 8-inch square baking pan.

2. In 1-quart saucepan, heat water to boiling over high heat. Remove from heat; stir in dates, instant coffee, and baking soda. Let stand 15 minutes.

3. Meanwhile, in small bowl, combine flour, cocoa, baking powder, and salt. In large bowl, with mixer at medium-high speed, beat 3 tablespoons butter and granulated sugar until creamy. Add egg and vanilla; beat until blended. Reduce speed to low. Alternately add flour mixture and date mixture, beginning and ending with flour mixture; beat just until batter is blended, occasionally scraping bowl with rubber spatula (batter will be thin).

4. Pour batter into prepared pan; spread evenly. Bake until toothpick inserted in center comes out clean, 18 to 20 minutes.

5. Meanwhile, in clean 1-quart saucepan, combine brown sugar, cream, and remaining 2 tablespoons butter; heat to boiling over medium heat, stirring frequently. Boil 1 minute, stirring. Remove from heat.

6. Remove pudding from oven. Turn oven control to broil. Pour brown-sugar mixture over hot pudding; spread evenly. Return pudding to oven; broil at closest position to heat source until bubbly, about 30 seconds. Cool in pan on wire rack 15 minutes. Serve warm with whipped cream, if you like.

Each serving: About 170 calories, 2g protein, 28g carbohydrate, 6g total fat (4g saturated), 34mg cholesterol, 175mg sodium.

Jeweled Chocolate Terrines

This makes a great dessert cut into 3/4-inch slices and dolloped with whipped cream. For a decadent candy, cut each slice into quarters and dust with cocoa.

PREP: 45 MINUTES PLUS CHILLING   COOK: 10 MINUTES
MAKES 6 MINI TERRINES OR 24 SERVINGS

2 2/3 cups heavy or whipping cream
2 pounds semisweet chocolate bars
   or 4 packages (32 squares)
   semisweet chocolate, chopped
1 cup dried tart cherries (4 ounces)
1 cup dried apricots (4 ounces),
   chopped

1/3 cup almond-flavored liqueur
2 cups hazelnuts (filberts; 8 ounces),
   toasted and skinned (page 97)
1 cup shelled pistachios (about 8
   ounces unshelled), lightly toasted
whipped cream (optional)

1. Line six 5 3/4" by 3 1/4" mini metal loaf pans with foil, allowing foil to extend over rims of pans and pressing out as many wrinkles as possible.
2. In 2-quart saucepan, heat cream to boiling over medium-high heat. Place chocolate in large bowl. Pour hot cream over chocolate; stir constantly until chocolate has melted.
3. In small microwave-safe bowl, combine cherries, apricots, and liqueur. Microwave on High 30 seconds to soften fruit.
4. Stir nuts and fruit-liqueur mixture into chocolate mixture until well combined. Pour chocolate mixture into prepared pans. Cover and refrigerate until firm, at least 4 hours. Tightly cover with foil. Refrigerate up to 1 month.
5. To serve, remove terrines from pans; peel off foil. Cut into slices and serve with whipped cream, if desired.

Each serving: About 420 calories, 6g protein, 35g carbohydrate, 31g total fat (14g saturated), 37mg cholesterol, 10mg sodium.

Chocolate Éclairs

Why buy éclairs? Nothing can compare to your first bite of a freshly prepared éclair made right at home.

PREP: 1 HOUR PLUS CHILLING, COOLING, AND STANDING   BAKE: 40 MINUTES
MAKES ABOUT 30 ÉCLAIRS

CHOCOLATE PASTRY CREAM
2 1/4 cups milk
3 squares (3 ounces) semisweet
   chocolate, chopped
1 squares (1 ounce) unsweetened
   chocolate, chopped
4 large egg yolks
2/3 cup sugar
1/4 cup all-purpose flour
1/4 cup cornstarch
1 tablespoon vanilla extract

CHOUX PASTRY
1/2 cup butter or margarine
   (1 stick), cut into pieces
1 cup water
1/4 teaspoon salt
1 cup all-purpose flour
4 large eggs

CHOCOLATE GLAZE
3 squares (3 ounces) semisweet
   chocolate, chopped
3 tablespoons heavy or whipping
   cream

1. Prepare Chocolate Pastry Cream: In 3-quart saucepan, heat 2 cups milk over medium-high heat until bubbles form around edge.
2. In 1-quart saucepan, melt semisweet and unsweetened chocolates, stirring frequently, until smooth. Meanwhile, in large bowl, with wire whisk, beat egg yolks, remaining 1/4 cup milk, and sugar until combined; whisk in flour and cornstarch until blended. Gradually whisk hot milk into egg-yolk mixture. Return milk mixture to saucepan; cook over medium-high heat, whisking constantly, until mixture has thickened and boils. Reduce heat to low and cook, stirring, 2 minutes.
3. Remove from heat; stir in melted chocolate and vanilla until blended. Pour pastry cream into shallow dish. Press plastic wrap directly onto surface. Refrigerate until cool, at least 2 hours or up to overnight.
4. Preheat oven to 400°F. Grease and flour large cookie sheet.
5. Prepare Choux Pastry: In 3-quart saucepan, combine butter, water, and salt; heat over medium-high heat until butter has melted and mixture boils. Remove from heat. Add flour all at once; with wooden spoon, vigorously stir until mixture leaves side of pan and forms a ball. Add eggs to flour mixture, one at a time, beating well after each addition, until mixture is smooth and satiny.

210 Desserts

6. Spoon dough into large pastry bag fitted with 1/2-inch plain tip. Pipe dough in lengths about 3½ inches long and 3/4 inch wide, 1 inch apart, on prepared cookie sheet to make about 30 éclairs. With moistened finger, gently smooth tops.

7. Bake until golden, about 40 minutes. Remove éclairs from oven; with tip of knife, make small slit in end of each éclair to release steam. Return éclairs to oven; let stand 10 minutes. Transfer éclairs to wire racks to cool completely.

8. With small knife, make hole in one end of each éclair. Whisk pastry cream until smooth; spoon into clean large pastry bag fitted with 1/4-inch plain tip. Pipe pastry cream into éclairs.

9. Prepare Chocolate Glaze: In 6-inch skillet or 1-quart saucepan, combine chocolate and cream; heat over low heat, stirring frequently, until chocolate has melted and mixture is smooth. Remove from heat. Dip top of each éclair into chocolate mixture, smoothing with small metal spatula if necessary. Let stand on wire racks until chocolate sets.

Each éclair: About 116 calories, 3g protein, 12g carbohydrate, 6g total fat (1g saturated), 70mg cholesterol, 70mg sodium.

CHOUX PASTRY

Choux pastry dough is unique because it is cooked twice: first on the stove and then in the oven. The dough makes a light, airy, hollow pastry that is perfect for filling with ice cream, whipped cream, or pastry cream.

• **When cooking the dough, be sure the butter is completely melted by the time the water comes to a full boil.** If too much water evaporates, the dough will be dry.

• **For the highest puff, always shape and bake choux pastry dough while it's still warm.**

• **Bake the pastries until golden brown:** Pale undercooked pastries collapse when removed from the oven.

• **Choux dough creates a lot of steam when baked:** This steam needs to be released or the pastries will become soggy. As soon as the pastries are removed from the oven, use the tip of a small knife to cut a slit into the side of each one.

• **Unfilled choux dough pastries can be frozen in heavy-duty ziptight plastic bags for up to one month;** simply crisp in a 400°F oven for a few minutes before serving.

FROZEN DESSERTS

Chocolate Ice Cream

This ice cream is truly an intense eating experience, thanks to a generous amount of unsweetened and semisweet chocolates and its very rich vanilla ice-cream base.

Prep: 10 minutes plus chilling and freezing   Cook: 20 minutes
Makes about 6 cups or 12 servings

3 cups half-and-half or light cream
4 large egg yolks
3/4 cup sugar
1/8 teaspoon salt
1 cup heavy or whipping cream
1 teaspoon vanilla extract
3 squares (3 ounces) unsweetened chocolate, chopped
2 squares (2 ounces) semisweet chocolate, chopped

1. In heavy 3-quart saucepan, heat half-and-half to boiling over medium-high heat.
2. Meanwhile, in medium bowl, with wire whisk, whisk egg yolks, sugar, and salt until smooth. Gradually whisk half-and-half into egg-yolk mixture. Return mixture to saucepan; cook over medium heat, stirring constantly, just until mixture coats back of spoon (do not boil, or it will curdle). Remove from heat. Strain custard through sieve into large bowl; add 3/4 cup heavy cream and vanilla.
3. In heavy 2-quart saucepan, melt unsweetened and semisweet chocolates with remaining 1/4 cup cream over low heat, stirring frequently, until smooth. Stir 1 cup ice-cream mixture into chocolate mixture; stir back into ice-cream mixture. Press plastic wrap onto surface of custard. Refrigerate until well chilled, at least 2 hours or up to overnight.
4. Freeze in ice-cream maker as manufacturer directs.

Each serving: About 277 calories, 4g protein, 21g carbohydrate, 21g total fat (13g saturated), 120mg cholesterol, 61mg sodium.

Chocolate Sorbet

When you want a frozen chocolate dessert that is a bit lighter than ice cream, sorbet is a good choice. This one packs plenty of satisfying chocolate flavor.

PREP: 10 MINUTES PLUS CHILLING AND FREEZING   COOK: 12 MINUTES
MAKES ABOUT 4 CUPS OR 8 SERVINGS

3/4 cup sugar
2 1/2 cups water
2 squares (2 ounces) unsweetened
  chocolate, chopped

1/4 cup light corn syrup
1 1/2 teaspoons vanilla extract

1. In 2-quart saucepan, combine sugar and water; heat to boiling over high heat, stirring until sugar has dissolved. Reduce heat to medium; cook 3 minutes. Remove from heat.

2. In heavy 1-quart saucepan, heat chocolate and corn syrup over low heat, stirring frequently, until chocolate has melted and mixture is smooth.

3. With wire whisk, stir 1 cup sugar syrup into chocolate mixture until well blended. Stir chocolate mixture into remaining sugar syrup in saucepan; stir in vanilla. Pour into medium bowl; cover and refrigerate until well chilled, about 1 1/2 hours.

4. Freeze in ice-cream maker as manufacturer directs.

Each serving: About 141 calories, 1g protein, 29g carbohydrate, 4g total fat (2g saturated), 0mg cholesterol, 14mg sodium.

Rocky Road Ice Cream Cake

This ooey-gooey treat is like a big sundae made in a springform pan. It's prepared with chocolate ice cream, our secret Fudge Sauce (which is delicious spooned over a bowl of vanilla ice cream), cookies, peanuts, and miniature marshmallows. If you run short on time, jarred fudge sauce will do just fine.

PREP: 30 MINUTES PLUS CHILLING AND FREEZING   COOK: 8 MINUTES
MAKES 14 SERVINGS

FUDGE SAUCE
1 cup heavy or whipping cream
3/4 cup sugar
4 squares (4 ounces) unsweetened
    chocolate, chopped
2 tablespoons light corn syrup
2 tablespoons butter or margarine
2 teaspoons vanilla extract

ROCKY ROAD CAKE
2 pints chocolate ice cream,
    softened
14 chocolate sandwich cookies
2 cups miniature marshmallows
1 cup salted peanuts,
    coarsely chopped

1. Prepare Fudge Sauce: In heavy 2-quart saucepan, combine cream, sugar, chocolate, and corn syrup. Heat to boiling over medium heat, stirring occasionally. Cook over medium-low heat, stirring constantly, until sauce thickens slightly, 4 minutes longer. Remove from heat. Add butter and vanilla; stir until butter has melted and sauce is smooth and glossy. Cover surface of sauce with plastic wrap; refrigerate until cool, about 2 hours. Makes about 1 2/3 cups.

2. When sauce is cool, assemble Rocky Road Cake: Wrap outside of 9" by 3" springform pan with foil. Spoon 1 pint softened chocolate ice cream into pan. Cover ice cream with plastic wrap; press down to spread ice cream evenly and eliminate air pockets; remove plastic wrap. Insert cookies, upright, into ice cream to form a ring around side of pan, making sure to push cookie to pan bottom. Sprinkle 1 cup marshmallows and 1/2 cup peanuts over ice cream; gently press in with hand.

3. Spoon remaining ice cream over marshmallows and peanuts. Place plastic wrap on ice cream and spread evenly; remove plastic. Spread 2/3 cup Fudge Sauce over ice cream (if sauce is too firm, microwave briefly to soften but do not reheat); reserve remaining sauce. Sprinkle remaining marshmallows and peanuts over sauce; press in gently with hand. Cover cake with plastic wrap and freeze until firm, at least 6 hours.

4. To serve, uncover cake and remove foil. Wrap towels dampened with warm water around side of pan for about 20 seconds to slightly soften ice cream. Remove side of pan and place cake on cake stand or plate. Let stand at room temperature about 10 minute for easier slicing. Meanwhile, place remaining Fudge Sauce in microwave-safe bowl. Heat in microwave oven, uncovered, on High 30 to 40 seconds or until hot, stirring once. Serve hot sauce to spoon over cake, if you like.

Each serving: About 365 calories, 7g protein, 36g carbohydrate, 23g total fat (11g saturated), 77mg cholesterol, 220mg sodium.

Brownie Baked Alaska

You'll love our new take on this classic dessert. Vanilla ice cream with cherries and chocolate is layered between fudgy brownies and topped with dark cocoa meringue. You can assemble the ice-cream loaf and freeze it for up to two weeks. About thirty minutes before serving, prepare the meringue, spread it over the frozen loaf, and pop it into the oven until the meringue peaks are lightly browned.

PREP: 55 MINUTES PLUS COOLING AND FREEZING   BAKE: 30 MINUTES
MAKES 12 SERVINGS

BROWNIE LAYERS
6 tablespoons butter or margarine
2 squares (2 ounces) unsweetened
  chocolate, chopped
2 squares (2 ounces) semisweet
  chocolate, chopped
3/4 cup granulated sugar
1 1/2 teaspoons vanilla extract
1/4 teaspoon salt
2 large eggs
1/2 cup all-purpose flour

2 pints vanilla ice cream with
  cherries and fudge flakes, softened

COCOA MERINGUE
1/4 cup confectioners' sugar
1/4 cup unsweetened cocoa
2 tablespoons plus 2 teaspoons
  pasteurized powdered egg whites
  (such as Just Whites)
1/2 cup warm water
pinch salt
1/4 cup granulated sugar

1. Prepare Brownie Layers: Preheat oven to 350°F. Grease 8-inch square baking pan. Line pan with foil; grease foil and dust with flour.

2. In heavy 2-quart saucepan, melt butter and semisweet and unsweetened chocolates over low heat, stirring frequently, until smooth. Remove from heat. With wooden spoon, stir in sugar, vanilla, and salt. Stir in eggs until well mixed. Stir in flour just until blended. Spread batter evenly in prepared pan.

3. Bake 25 minutes (toothpick inserted in center will not come out clean). Cool completely in pan on wire rack. When cool, invert onto cutting board; peel off foil. Cut brownie in half.

4. Line 8 1/2" by 4 1/2" by 2 1/2" metal loaf pan with plastic wrap. Press one brownie layer into bottom of pan. Spoon ice cream over brownie; spread into a smooth, even layer. Top with remaining brownie. Cover pan with plastic wrap and freeze until firm, at least 4 hours.

5. About 30 minutes before serving, preheat oven to 475°F. Prepare

Cocoa Meringue: In small bowl, sift confectioners' sugar and cocoa. In large bowl, with wire whisk, gently mix powdered egg whites and warm water until mixture is well blended and egg whites have dissolved. Stir in salt. With mixer at medium speed, beat egg whites until frothy. Increase speed to high; sprinkle in granulated sugar, 2 tablespoons at a time, beating until sugar has dissolved and egg whites stand in stiff, glossy peaks when beaters are lifted. With rubber spatula, gently fold cocoa mixture into egg whites, one-third at a time, until evenly blended.

6. Remove plastic wrap from top of loaf. Invert loaf onto oven-safe platter; remove remaining plastic wrap. Spread Cocoa Meringue over top and sides of loaf, swirling with spatula to form peaks and making sure meringue extends onto dish to completely seal in ice cream and brownie. Bake until meringue peaks are lightly browned, 3 to 4 minutes. Serve immediately.

Each serving: About 385 calories, 8g protein, 45g carbohydrate, 21g total fat (14g saturated), 98mg cholesterol, 187mg sodium.

Brownie Sundae Cups

What could be better than brownie cupcakes filled with scoops of vanilla ice cream and drizzled with fudge sauce. Both the brownies and sauce can be prepared hours ahead. Assemble the sundaes just before serving.

PREP: 20 MINUTES PLUS COOLING BAKE: 30 MINUTES
MAKES 6 SERVINGS

BROWNIE CUPS
1 cup all-purpose flour
1/2 cup unsweetened cocoa
1 teaspoon baking powder
1/4 teaspoon salt
3/4 cup butter or margarine
   (1 1/2 sticks)
1 1/2 cups sugar
3 large eggs
2 teaspoons vanilla extract

HOT FUDGE SAUCE
1/2 cup sugar
1/3 cup unsweetened cocoa
1/4 cup heavy or whipping cream
2 tablespoons butter or margarine,
   cut in pieces
1 teaspoon vanilla extract

1 pint vanilla ice cream

1. Preheat oven to 350°F. Grease 6 jumbo muffin-pan cups (about 4" by 2" each) or six 6-ounce custard cups.

2. Prepare Brownie Cups: In medium bowl, combine flour, cocoa, baking powder, and salt. In 3-quart saucepan, melt butter over medium-low heat. Remove from heat; stir in sugar. Add eggs and vanilla; stir until well mixed. Stir in flour mixture just until blended. Spoon batter evenly into prepared muffin-pan cups.

3. Bake until toothpick inserted in center comes out almost clean, 30 to 35 minutes. Cool in pan on wire rack 5 minutes. Run tip of thin knife around brownies to loosen from sides of pan. Invert brownies onto rack; cool 10 minutes longer to serve warm, or cool completely to serve later.

4. While Brownie Cups are cooling, prepare Hot Fudge Sauce: In heavy 1-quart saucepan, combine sugar, cocoa, cream, and butter; heat to boiling over medium-high heat, stirring frequently. Remove from heat; stir in vanilla. Serve sauce warm, or cool completely, then cover and refrigerate up to 2 weeks. Gently reheat before using. Makes about 2/3 cup.

5. Assemble brownie sundaes: With small knife, cut 1 1/2- to 2-inch circle in center of each brownie; remove tops and set aside. Scoop out brownie centers, making sure not to cut through bottoms of brownies. Transfer brownie centers to small bowl; reserve to sprinkle over ice cream another

day. Place each Brownie Cup on dessert plate. Scoop ice cream into Brownie Cups and drizzle with Hot Fudge Sauce; replace brownie tops.

Each serving without sauce: About 500 calories, 7g protein, 61g carbohydrate, 28g total fat (16g saturated), 152mg cholesterol, 355mg sodium.

Each tablespoon fudge sauce: About 80 calories, 1g protein, 10g carbohydrate, 5g total fat (3g saturated), 14mg cholesterol, 25mg sodium.